Animal
Rights

Animal Rights

OTHER BOOKS IN THE HISTORY OF ISSUES SERIES:

The Death Penalty
Euthanasia
Evolution
Terrorism

Animal Rights

Nick Treanor, *Book Editor*

Bruce Glassman, *Vice President*
Bonnie Szumski, *Publisher*
Helen Cothran, *Managing Editor*

GREENHAVEN PRESS
An imprint of Thomson Gale, a part of The Thomson Corporation

Detroit • New York • San Francisco • San Diego • New Haven, Conn.
Waterville, Maine • London • Munich

For more information, contact
Greenhaven Press
27500 Drake Rd.
Farmington Hills, MI 48331-3535
Or you can visit our Internet site at http://www.gale.com

LIBRARY OF CONGRESS CATALOGING-IN-PUBLICATION DATA

Animal rights / Nick Treanor, book editor.
  p. cm. — (The history of issues)
Includes bibliographical references and index.
  ISBN 0-7377-1905-2 (lib. : alk. paper) — ISBN 0-7377-1906-0 (pbk. : alk. paper)
  1. Animal rights. 2. Animal rights—History. I. Treanor, Nick. II. Series.
HV4708.A54 2005
179'.3—dc22

2003067680

Printed in the United States of America

Contents

Foreword   12
Introduction   15

Chapter 1: The Early Humane Movement

1. **If Humans Have Rights, Animals Have Rights**   28
   by Henry Salt
   The traditional arguments against extending
   rights to animals fail. Animals have rights because, like people, they are individuals who
   deserve to live their lives freely.

2. **Animal Experimentation Is Cruel to Animals and to Human Beings**   35
   by Enid Widdrington
   It is wrong for science to inflict suffering on
   animals. It harms animals and it diminishes
   the quality of human life.

3. **The Rise of Legal Protection for Animals**   42
   by Roswell McCrea
   The first anticruelty legislation was passed in
   England in 1822. It soon spread to the United
   States and by 1910 every state had laws pro-
   tecting animals from cruelty.

4. **Experiments on Animals Are Justified**   51
   by Walter Bradford Cannon
   Experiments on animals were crucial to many
   of the medical discoveries of the late 1800s
   and early 1900s. Those who oppose such experiments know little about them.

Chapter 2: Philosophical Debates over Animal Rights

1. A Moral Protest Is Born 61
by James M. Jasper and Dorothy Nelkin
The animal rights movement had few supporters and little respectability until philosopher
Peter Singer argued that animals deserve
moral consideration. He was soon joined by
another philosopher, Tom Regan, who made
an even stronger case for animal rights.

2. Equality for Animals 72
by Peter Singer
Animals deserve to be treated with equal consideration because they can feel pleasure and
pain. It is this ability, rather than race, sex, intelligence, or species membership, that matters morally.

3. Humans Should Be Biased Toward Humans 82
by William Timberlake
Humans are justified in giving preferential
treatment to other humans because humans
share DNA. Without such preferential treatment, the species could not survive.

4. Animals Have Inherent Value 87
by Tom Regan
Animals, like people, have inherent value.
They have rights that cannot be violated because they have lives that matter to them.

5. Animal Rights Are Weaker than Human Rights 100
by Mary Anne Warren
Tom Regan's theory relies on an obscure notion of inherent value and entails that every
being either has rights equal to our own or
has no rights at all. Animals do have rights,

but they are weaker than human rights because animals lack rationality.

6. Animals Feel Pleasure and Pain   109
by David DeGrazia
A careful consideration of the evidence suggests that animals do in fact have the capacity to feel pleasure and pain.

7. Animal Rights Are Easy to Recognize but Hard to Respect   119
by Robert Wright
The logic behind animal rights is persuasive. Because animals cannot press for reform themselves, however, it is much harder for human beings to respect animal rights.

Chapter 3: Animal Rights Activism

1. The Public Debate over Animal Experimentation   134
by Newsweek
The public increasingly recognizes that animal experimentation raises a moral quandary. The debate between scientists and activists has led to reforms, but the deep moral questions remain unanswered.

2. An Animal Rights Platform   146
by the Animal Rights Network
Animal rights activists are committed to achieving the following twelve goals, which involve ending the exploitation of animals and preserving the integrity of their lives and habitats.

3. Extreme Tactics Have Saved Countless Animals   150
by No Compromise
The most effective way to save animals is through direct action against the individuals and companies that harm them. The lab raids

of the 1980s also pushed the issue of animal rights into the public eye.

4. Illegal Tactics in Defense of Animals Are Sometimes Justified 161
by Peter Singer
Although citizens in a democracy must always exhaust legal options first, there are times when illegal actions in defense of moral goals are justified.

5. The Use of Violence in Support of Animal Rights Is Wrong 168
by Jerry Simonelli
Those who advocate for animal rights should follow the example of Mohandas Gandhi and Martin Luther King Jr., and denounce violent tactics.

6. Animal Rights Terrorism 173
by Wesley J. Smith
The animal rights movement increasingly relies on terrorism, as radical groups advocate violence and property destruction. Even mainstream organizations are involved.

Chapter 4: Animal Rights and Scientific Progress

1. Scientists Have Responded by Using Fewer Animals 179
by the Economist
Scientists have responded to animal rights concerns by using fewer animals and by developing alternatives to animal experimentation.

2. The Benefits of Animal Research Are Worth the Cost 189
by Carl Cohen
The good that is produced by animal experimentation outweighs the bad that is involved

in such research. Because of this, it is not wrong to experiment on animals.

3. Science Helping Animals   195
by David Barboza

Scientists used to be the enemies of animal rights. Today, scientific research into animal welfare is helping change animal treatment standards in the food industry.

Chronology   201
Organizations to Contact   206
For Further Research   211
Index   215

Foreword

In the 1940s, at the height of the Holocaust, Jews struggled to create a nation of their own in Palestine, a region of the Middle East that at the time was controlled by Britain. The British had placed limits on Jewish immigration to Palestine, hampering efforts to provide refuge to Jews fleeing the Holocaust. In response to this and other British policies, an underground Jewish resistance group called Irgun began carrying out terrorist attacks against British targets in Palestine, including immigration, intelligence, and police offices. Most famously, the group bombed the King David Hotel in Jerusalem, the site of a British military headquarters. Although the British were warned well in advance of the attack, they failed to evacuate the building. As a result, ninety-one people were killed (including fifteen Jews) and forty-five were injured.

Early in the twentieth century, Ireland, which had long been under British rule, was split into two countries. The south, populated mostly by Catholics, eventually achieved independence and became the Republic of Ireland. Northern Ireland, mostly Protestant, remained under British control. Catholics in both the north and south opposed British control of the north, and the Irish Republican Army (IRA) sought unification of Ireland as an independent nation. In 1969, the IRA split into two factions. A new radical wing, the Provisional IRA, was created and soon undertook numerous terrorist bombings and killings throughout Northern Ireland, the Republic of Ireland, and even in England. One of its most notorious attacks was the 1974 bombing of a Birmingham, England, bar that killed nineteen people.

In the mid-1990s, an Islamic terrorist group called al Qaeda began carrying out terrorist attacks against American targets overseas. In communications to the media, the organization listed several complaints against the United States. It generally opposed all U.S. involvement and presence in the Middle East. It particularly objected to the presence of U.S. troops in Saudi Arabia, which is the home of several Islamic holy sites. And it strongly condemned the United States for supporting the nation of Israel, which it claimed was an oppressor of Muslims. In 1998 al Qaeda's leaders issued a fatwa (a religious legal statement) calling for Muslims to kill Americans. Al Qaeda acted on this order many times—most memorably on September 11, 2001, when it attacked the World Trade Center and the Pentagon, killing nearly three thousand people.

These three groups—Irgun, the Provisional IRA, and al Qaeda—have achieved varied results. Irgun's terror campaign contributed to Britain's decision to pull out of Palestine and to support the creation of Israel in 1948. The Provisional IRA's tactics kept pressure on the British, but they also alienated many would-be supporters of independence for Northern Ireland. Al Qaeda's attacks provoked a strong U.S. military response but did not lessen America's involvement in the Middle East nor weaken its support of Israel. Despite these different results, the means and goals of these groups were similar. Although they emerged in different parts of the world during different eras and in support of different causes, all three had one thing in common: They all used clandestine violence to undermine a government they deemed oppressive or illegitimate.

The destruction of oppressive governments is not the only goal of terrorism. For example, terror is also used to minimize dissent in totalitarian regimes and to promote extreme ideologies. However, throughout history the motivations of terrorists have been remarkably similar, proving the old adage that "the more things change, the more they remain the same." Arguments for and against terrorism thus boil down to the same set of universal arguments regardless of the age: Some argue that terrorism is justified to change (or, in the case of state terror, to maintain) the prevailing political order; others respond that terrorism is inhumane and unacceptable under any circumstances. These basic views transcend time and place.

Similar fundamental arguments apply to other controversial social issues. For instance, arguments over the death penalty have always featured competing views of justice. Scholars cite biblical texts to claim that a person who takes a life must forfeit his or her life, while others cite religious doctrine to support their view that only God can take a human life. These arguments have remained essentially the same throughout the centuries. Likewise, the debate over euthanasia has persisted throughout the history of Western civilization. Supporters argue that it is compassionate to end the suffering of the dying by hastening their impending death; opponents insist that it is society's duty to make the dying as comfortable as possible as death takes its natural course.

Greenhaven Press's The History of Issues series illustrates this constancy of arguments surrounding major social issues. Each volume in the series focuses on one issue—including terrorism, the death penalty, and euthanasia—and examines how the debates have both evolved and remained essentially the same over the years. Primary documents such as newspaper articles, speeches, and government reports illuminate historical developments and offer perspectives from throughout history. Secondary sources provide overviews and commentaries from a more contemporary perspective. An introduction begins each anthology and supplies essential context and background. An annotated table of contents, chronology, and index allow for easy reference, and a bibliography and list of organizations to contact point to additional sources of information on the book's topic. With these features, The History of Issues series permits readers to glimpse both the historical and contemporary dimensions of humanity's most pressing and controversial social issues.

Introduction

A couple of generations ago, a thorough search through even a good library would have turned up few books dealing with animal rights. Perhaps the better universities would have had a copy of Henry Salt's seminal 1892 work *Animals' Rights*, but for the most part any books that had to do with rights had to do with human rights. Today the situation could not be more different. There are hundreds of books on animal rights, dozens of major nonprofit organizations working to either promote or refute animal rights, and even special centers at some law schools devoted to animal rights law. The rise to prominence of animal rights as an issue was not, however, as sudden as it may appear to be. Rather, the contemporary focus on animal rights reflects a general, historical broadening of a Western view on animals. As beliefs about animals have changed, so too has the common conception of how they deserve to be treated.

There is no such thing as *the* traditional view of animals, for different cultures have historically held very different attitudes towards animals. We do have reason to believe, however, that the earliest human attitude toward animals was one of great respect. Paleolithic cave paintings of Europe, which date back as far as 30,000 B.C. and serve as one of the most important sources of knowledge of early human culture, tend to focus in their artistic depictions on animals, and in particular on large mammals such as mammoths, bison, wild horses, and cattle. Scholars suggest that the preliterate peoples responsible for these artistic representations viewed animals in much the same way that contemporary hunting and gathering societies do—as living, physical embodiments of spiritual beings. As James Serpell, a professor of animal welfare at the University of Pennsylvania School of

Veterinary Medicine, notes, such beliefs influenced how primitive cultures believed animals should be treated:

> The idea that animals are fully conscious beings who possess spiritual power is widespread among hunting and gathering societies. Not surprisingly, it also appears to engender considerable anxiety and guilt about killing animals for food. Most of these cultures engage in complex rituals and taboos designed either to relieve the guilt arising from hunting or to honor the spirit of deceased animals.[1]

According to Serpell, human attitudes towards animals shifted radically with the advent of agriculture about 15,000 years ago. Although humans had long depended on animals for food, animals had been seen as independent and equal in important ways to human beings. Human settlement, agriculture, and domestication shifted the balance of power sharply in favor of humans, however, and, as Serpell says, "animals became slaves or subordinates, entirely dependent on humans for care and protection."[2]

Although the early respect for animal life survived in some cultures, most notably in the East, where Buddhism, Jainism, and the yogic branches of Hinduism emphasize respect for all living things, it did not in the West. Instead, the dominant view in the West emphasized that humans had dominion over animals, that is, that animals are human property. There were several sources for this idea. Early Christian thinkers insisted on a sharp distinction between humans and animals, contending that only humans have souls. They also quoted with approval Genesis 1:28, the biblical verse according to which Adam and Eve were granted "dominion over the fish of the sea and over the birds of the air and over every living thing that moves upon the earth." Another important influence was Aristotle (384–322 B.C.), who had conceived of nature as a scale of creation in which lesser beings were created for the use of those higher up the scale. Similarly, Aristotle's emphasis on the importance of rationality to moral status left animals outside the domain of moral concern. Finally, after the Enlightenment, humans, it was thought, had rights and could own property, but animals had no rights and could not own property. Similarly, Enlightenment thinkers stressed the injustice of human slavery (the owning of humans), but said nothing against the owning of animals.

The modern development of animal rights as an issue, which has two phases, is rooted in this historical conception of animals as human property. The first phase started roughly in the mid-1800s, and emphasized what is known as animal welfare, or the humane treatment of animals. The second phase developed only much later, in the 1970s, and granted animals much greater moral status. Both of these phases developed out of a view of animals as under the control and protection of human beings. The main difference is that the first phase largely accepted that animals are human property, and argued in essence that human ownership of animals involves responsibility for humane treatment. The second phase, in contrast, rejected the very idea that animals are human property and argued that animals are full members of the moral community.

The Prevention of Cruelty

Concern for animals in modern times first took expression in laws against cruelty. The first known law forbidding cruelty was Martin's Act, passed by the British parliament in 1822. The parliament had rejected a similar bill in 1800, but this time saw fit to "prevent cruel and unusual treatment" of cattle and most other farm and draft animals. Successive laws in 1835, 1849, and 1854 extended protection to all domesticated mammals, including pets. Like the laws that would be passed a half century later in the United States, the British laws focused only on *cruelty*, which was understood to be excessive or wanton abuse. As far as the law was concerned there was nothing the matter with harming animals, so long as the harm was not needless. Thus, for instance, what the laws ruled out was not the working of animals for human benefit, nor even the killing of animals, but rather such practices as beating animals excessively or for no good reason.

The British also pioneered the development of humane societies, which worked to ensure laws protecting animals were enforced and generally promoted humane treatment of animals. In 1824, the Society for the Prevention of Cruelty to Animals was formed in England; the United States got its own version forty years later when Henry Bergh founded the American Society for the Prevention of Cruelty to Animals. (It was joined, in 1877, by the American Humane Society.) The groups quickly grew in stature and influence, and by 1907, every American state had an anticruelty statute. Again, the focus tended to be on promoting better treatment of animals rather than on ending all forms of animal use or exploitation.

One issue that was of particular prominence around the turn of the century was that of vivisection, or animal experimentation. Although there was not yet a huge research industry for drugs and other treatments involving animals, live animals were often used, without anesthetic, in research studies into basic physiology and in public demonstrations of well-known physiological facts. Antivivisectionists tended to be especially opposed to these latter experiments, in which animals suffered tremendous pain for arguably minimal human benefit. For instance, in some cases scientists would stimulate the raw nerve endings of dogs, causing them to howl in pain, merely to demonstrate to spectators how the central nervous system works.

Although there were notable exceptions, most of those in the early humane and antivivisectionist movement shared the dominant view that God had granted humans dominion over animals. They understood this dominion to be one of stewardship; although God had, in their view, given humans control over animals, humans were obliged to use this control responsibly and compassionately. Typical, for instance, was the position of Lord Shaftesbury, a prominent British social activist in the 1800s, who wrote in a letter, "I was convinced that God had called me to devote whatever advantages He might have bestowed upon me to the cause of the weak, the helpless, both man and beast, and those who have none to help them."[3]

The Issue Resurfaces

If the beginning of the first phase of the development of the issue of animal rights is dated to 1822, the year of Martin's Act, the second phase can be said to have begun nearly 150 years later. The second phase differs from the first in that it challenged the idea that humans are to have dominion over animals. Once again, the birthplace of the new ideas was Britain. In an article published in the *Sunday Times*, British author and social critic Brigid Brophy inaugurated a new ethical sensibility towards animals. Brophy argued not that humans should treat animals well in exchange for having control over them, but that animals, like humans, have inalienable rights. In 1969, Brophy contacted Richard Ryder, an Oxford psychologist who had begun publishing critiques of animal abuse, and the pair soon joined three young philosophers at Oxford, John Harris and Roslind and Stanley Godlovitch. Within a couple of years Ryder and the Godlovitches published *Animals, Men, and Morals*, a collection of essays that was the first serious academic work on the issue of animal rights since Henry Salt's *Animals' Rights* in 1892.

Also at Oxford at the time was a young lecturer from Australia who would go on to become perhaps the most influential modern thinker on the issue of animal rights. Peter Singer's review of *Animals, Men, and Morals* in the *New York Review of Books* in 1973 made such a good case for the main line of thought behind the edited collection that he was asked to publish a book of his own on the topic. This he did in 1975, with *Animal Liberation*, a bestselling book widely credited with bringing the issue of animal rights into the public eye.

Singer's book was a mix of intellectual research and activism; in addition to providing a solid theory of why it is wrong to harm animals, the book extensively catalogued the harm done to animals in scientific experiments and factory farming and included many suggestions on what readers could actually do to reduce animal suffering. Also, unlike many scholarly works, Singer's book was relatively engaging to read. For these reasons, perhaps, Singer's book became the handbook of animal rights activists. It is likely that most such activists had been drawn to the cause from a general sense of compassion towards animals; with *Animal Liberation* on their bookshelves, they had respectable intellectual backing for their heartfelt convictions.

Discriminating Against Animals

Singer argued, contrary to a long tradition in moral philosophy, that rationality does not matter to moral status. Rather, according to Singer, what matters is whether a being has the capacity to feel pleasure and pain. He pointed out that no one thinks that it is acceptable to hurt babies or severely retarded people just because they lack rationality, or the capacity for speech. If it is wrong to hurt babies and retarded people, Singer said, then it is wrong to hurt animals (or at least higher animals, such as mammals). To insist otherwise, Singer said, is speciesism, the view that human beings deserve higher regard simply because they are human. He compared this view with racism, according to which members of some races are judged to deserve better treatment simply because of their race, and with sexism, which holds that people deserve to be treated differently because of their sex. Singer insisted that species membership was, in itself, as morally irrelevant as race or sex. (To see what he is getting at, imagine we discovered a race of extraterrestrials that was just like us—they felt pleasure and pain, formed friendships and families, planned for their future, hoped their lives were meaningful, and so on. On Singer's view, the fact that these beings would not be members of the species *homo sapiens* is irrelevant to whether it would be wrong to hurt them.)

In advancing this argument, Singer was building on the thought of the English philosopher Jeremy Bentham, who had argued in 1789 that animals deserve to be treated equally by virtue of the fact that they are sentient. In a passage that concludes with a well-known question, Bentham wrote:

> The day *may* come when the rest of the animal creation may acquire those rights which never could have been withholden from them but by the hand of tyranny. The French have already discovered that the blackness of the skin is no reason why a human being should be abandoned without redress to the caprice of a tormentor. It may one day come to be recognised that the number of the legs, the villosity of the skin, or the termination of the *os sacrum* are reasons equally insufficient for abandoning a sensitive being to the same fate. What else is it that should trace the insuperable line? Is it the faculty of reason, or perhaps the faculty of discourse? But a full-grown horse or dog is beyond comparison a more rational, as well as a more conversable animal, than an infant of a day or a week or even a month old. But suppose they were otherwise, what would it avail? The question is not, Can they *reason*? nor Can they *talk*? but, Can they *suffer*?[4]

Equal Consideration of Interests

Singer did not merely argue that humans should not harm animals as freely as they do. He insisted that animals deserve equal moral consideration, which means not that they deserve to be treated exactly as humans are treated, but that they deserve to have their interests be given equal consideration. Although there will be many cases, he admits, in which it is difficult to judge the interests of animals, and difficult to make comparisons between animal interests and human interests, on his view it is obvious that we are morally obliged to treat animals much better than we do. People do derive some pleasure from eating meat, for example, but for Singer this small pleasure does not outweigh the harm done to animals (on factory farms and in the slaughterhouse). Singer's view thus allowed that although it is sometimes permissible to harm animals (when the benefits outweigh the costs), in most instances the harm humans cause animals is morally unjustified.

Although Singer's arguments were very influential, some of those who advocated better treatment for animals argued that they were mistaken. Singer's moral theory stopped short of granting animals *rights*, which are understood to be inviolable. Thus, for example, Singer thinks it is morally acceptable to perform a painful experiment on an animal if the benefits are great enough. His position is thus utilitarian: an act is morally permissible as long as it produces more good than bad. This view is very different from classical rights theory, which holds that if a creature has rights, it is wrong to violate those rights even if doing so would greatly benefit others. On this view, for instance, it would be wrong to kidnap people and perform experiments on them, even if doing so would greatly advance human knowledge, because doing so would violate their rights. Similarly, those who advocate animal rights, in the strict sense of the term rights, hold that animals have inviolable rights and that it is thus wrong to harm them even when doing so would produce great benefits. The most important advocate of this view is Tom Regan, whose 1984 book *The Case for Animal Rights* argues that animals have inviolable rights because they are what Regan calls "subjects of a life." Regan's book, perhaps because it is a tightly argued scholarly tract, never achieved the public success of Singer's book, but it was a significant contribution to the debate. (See Chapter Two of this anthology for articles by Singer and Regan, as well as by those opposed to them.)

The philosophical arguments of Singer, Regan, and others were as important to the development of the issue of animal rights as the arguments of John Locke and his contemporaries three centuries earlier had been to the development of the issue of human rights. But just as the ideas of the earlier philosophers were popularized by action in the streets (for instance, the French and American revolutions), there was a popular front to the issue of animal rights as well. It began in Britain in 1963 with the founding of the Hunt Sabateurs Association, which used confrontational tactics to disrupt traditional fox hunts in England. By 1972, the Animal Liberation Front, a loosely knit organization that advocated direct action against research institutes and factory farms, was active in the United Kingdom. Around the same time, more mainstream organizations, such as Greenpeace, emerged, and several high-profile campaigns captured the public imagination, swelled the ranks of existing organizations, and led to the founding of new ones. One of the most successful was Henry Spira's 1975 investigation into experiments on cats sponsored by the Museum of Natural History in New York City. After Spira, head of Animal Rights International, led protests against the experiments, which involved blinding, deafening, and mutiliating the sex organs of cats, the mayor of New York and 120 members of Congress opposed it and the National Institutes of Health cancelled its funding. Spira's group was also influential in curbing widespread use of the Draize test, in which solids or liquids are placed on the eyes of rabbits to test for causticity. Such campaigns popularized, at least in a rudimentary form, the issue of animal rights.

The heyday of animal rights activistism, however, was the 1980s, as dozens of national organizations emerged, including such giants as People for the Ethical Treatment of Animals (PETA), whose membership soared from 25 to over 250,000 within a few years. Dramatic rescues of research animals and undercover operations revealing the apparent horrors of animal research captured the limelight and increased the profile of animal rights groups. At the same time, though, more radical groups, especially the Animal Liberation Front (ALF), advocated violence and property destruction as a means to achieve their ends. They argued that the harm to animals justified extreme tactics and caused tens of millions of dollars in damage through arson, vandalism, and property destruction. As one anonymous member of the ALF was quoted as saying in an article by Steven Zak in the *Atlantic Monthly*, "I believe that you should do for others as you would have done for you. . . . If you were being used in painful experiments, you'd want someone to come to your rescue."[5]

New Era, New Issues

In the 1990s and the new century, the range of animal rights issues continued to broaden, as did the class of people concerned about the welfare of animals. Scientists had accepted that there were legitimate moral issues involved in animal experimentation and that, as Andrew Rowan put it in 1984, "It is just not adequate for scientists to argue that there is a quantum difference between the moral status of humans and animals if they are unable to give reasons for such a belief and defend their reasons in the arena of modern philosophical debate."[6]

The number of animals used in experiments thus dropped dramatically, as researchers looked for alternatives and avoided unnecessary studies. Although protests against research on animals continued, far more common were campaigns highlighting the issue of factory farms and promoting vegetarianism. These enjoyed considerable success, in part because of a growing concern about the health risks of diets high in red meat and animal fats. Although vegetarians remain a minority in North America, their numbers are significant and growing.

Most of the issues relevant to animal rights, such as the use of animals in science and for food and clothing, have been with us a very long time. At the start of the new century, however, there is one issue that is just beginning to emerge: the ethical issues involved in biotechnology. Most of the public focus has been on the moral issues involved concerning humans, most notably in stem cell research and the possibility of cloning. But the new biotechnology promises, or threatens, depending on your view, to greatly extend the ability of people to use animals for their purposes. One example is genetic engineering; the new technology will let scientists design animals to serve very specific purposes, especially in food production. Some envision a day in which such animals as chickens, pigs and cows are engineered to maximize meat production and minimize waste, even if that means producing animals that bear little resemblance to existing ones. Some see this as a terrifying possibility, including Andrew Linzey, who equates it to slavery and argues that there is "something morally sinister in the untrammelled development of genetic science which admits to no moral limits save that of the advancement of the controlling species."[7] Others, in constrast, think genetic engineering is a boon to both humans and animals. Humans can get all the meat they want, cheaply, while animals can be designed so that their natural desires and preferences are taken away, meaning they no longer suffer in intensive factory farm operations.

In *Animal Liberation*, the popular 1975 book often credited with kickstarting the modern animal rights movement, Peter Singer points out that originally only white men who owned property had rights. Gradually, he notes, this expanded so that everyone today recognizes that all people, regardless of race, or sex, or economic status, have rights that deserve to be recognized. Singer believes that recognition of the moral status of animals is the next logical step in the gradual expansion, since the Enlightenment, of the moral community. Nonetheless, he acknowledges that whatever similarities may exist between humans and animals, one difference is that animals cannot talk, and thus, unlike women and racial minorities, they cannot press for their own liberation. To those who believe animals have rights this is sometimes a reason for pessimism about the prospects for the universal recognition of animal rights. So too is the fact that the use of animals is, as Gary Francione, the director of the Animal Rights Law Center at Rutgers

University, points out, deeply integrated into our economy:

> The plain fact is that this country and other industrial countries are deeply dependent on animal exploitation to sustain their present economic structures. The plain fact is that we are more dependent on animal exploitation than were the states of the southern United States on human slavery. . . . So, although there are more people concerned about animals and the environment, little progress has been made because those who profit from animal exploitation and the government that exists to serve their interests have a lot to lose and are not budging—not an inch.[8]

For Francione, Singer, and others who think animals deserve better, the future is uncertain; although the rise of the issue of animal rights in the public consciousness has undeniably led to improvements in animal welfare, the chance for what Singer calls full liberation seems limited. To those who oppose the animal rights philosophy, in contrast, this is just as things should be.

Notes

1. James A. Serpell, "Pre-Christian Attitudes Toward Animals," *Encylopedia of Animal Rights and Animal Welfare*, ed. Marc Bekoff and Carron Meaney. Westport, CT: Greenwood Press, 1998, p. 76.
2. Serpell, "Pre-Christian Attitudes Toward Animals," p. 76.
3. Lord Shaftesbury, letter dated April 30, 1881, cited and discussed in Roberta Kalechofsky, *Between the Species: A Journal of Ethics,* Summer 1990, p. 160.
4. Jeremy Bentham, *Introduction to the Principles and Morals of Legislation*, 1789, p. 283.
5. Steven Zak, "Ethics and Animals," *Atlantic Monthly*, March 1989, p. 74.
6. Andrew N. Rowan, *Of Mice, Models, and Men: A Critical Analysis of Animal Research*. Albany: State University of New York Press, 1984, p. 260.
7. Andrew Linzey, "Genetic Engineering as Animal Slavery," in *Ethical Issues in Biotechnology*, ed. Richard Sherlock and John D. Morrey. New York: Rowman & Littlefield, 2002, p. 325.
8. Gary Francione, "Animal Rights: The Future," www.animal.law.org/commentaries/anmlrghtfut.htm.

THE
HISTORY
OF
ISSUES

CHAPTER 1

The Early Humane Movement

If Humans Have Rights, Animals Have Rights

HENRY SALT

Although his name is not widely known today, Englishman Henry Salt was one of the leading humanitarians of the nineteenth century. In the following excerpt from Animals' Rights, *one of nearly forty books he published, Salt argues that animals have rights as surely as people do. Salt considers and rejects two traditional arguments for the view that animals lack rights, and contends that animals have rights because they are individuals with lives that matter to them. Just as human beings deserve the liberty to live as they wish, animals deserve to be free from human interference, according to Salt.*

The immediate question that claims our attention is this—if men have rights, have animals their rights also?

From the earliest times there have been thinkers who, directly or indirectly, answered this question with an affirmative. The Buddhist and Pythagorean canons, dominated perhaps by the creed of reincarnation, included the maxim "not to kill or injure any innocent animal." The humanitarian philosophers of the Roman empire, among whom Seneca and Plutarch and Porphyry were the most conspicuous, took still higher ground in preaching humanity on the broadest principle of universal benevolence. "Since justice is due to rational beings," wrote Porphyry, "how is it possible to evade the admission that we are bound also

Henry Salt, *Animals' Rights: Considered in Relation to Social Progress*. New York: Macmillan & Co., 1894.

to act justly towards the races below us?"

It is a lamentable fact that during the churchdom of the middle ages, from the fourth century to the sixteenth, from the time of Porphyry to the time of [Michel de] Montaigne, little or no attention was paid to the question of the rights and wrongs of the lower races. Then, with the Reformation and the revival of learning, came a revival also of humanitarian feeling, as may be seen in many passages of [Desiderius] Erasmus and [Thomas] More, Shakespeare and [Francis] Bacon; but it was not until the eighteenth century, the age of enlightenment and "sensibility," of which Voltaire and [Jean-Jacques] Rousseau were the spokesmen, that the rights of animals obtained more deliberate recognition. From the great Revolution of 1789 dates the period when the world-wide spirit of humanitarianism, which had hitherto been felt by but one man in a million—the thesis of the philosopher or the vision of the poet—began to disclose itself, gradually and dimly at first, as an essential feature of democracy.

The Idea of Rights

A great and far-reaching effect was produced in England at this time by the publication of such revolutionary works as [Thomas] Paine's "Rights of Man," and Mary Wollstonecraft's "Vindication of the Rights of Women;" and looking back now, after the lapse of a hundred years, we can see that a still wider extension of the theory of rights was thenceforth inevitable. In fact, such a claim was anticipated—if only in bitter jest—by a contemporary writer, who furnishes us with a notable instance of how the mockery of one generation may become the reality of the next. There was published anonymously in 1792 a little volume entitled "A Vindication of the Rights of Brutes," a *reductio ad absurdum* of Mary Wollstonecraft's essay, written, as the author informs us, "to evince by demonstrative arguments the perfect equality of what is called the irrational species to the human." The further opinion is expressed that "after those wonderful productions of Mr. Paine and Mrs. Wollstonecraft, such a theory as the present seems to be necessary." It *was* necessary; and a very short term of years sufficed to bring it into effect; indeed, the theory had already been put forward by several English pioneers of nineteenth-century humanitarianism.

To Jeremy Bentham, in particular, belongs the high honour of first asserting the rights of animals with authority and persistence. "The legislator," he wrote,

> ought to interdict everything which may serve to lead to cruelty. The barbarous spectacles of gladiators no doubt contributed to give the Romans that ferocity which they displayed in their civil wars. A people accustomed to despise human life in their games could not be expected to respect it amid the fury of their passions. It is proper for the same reason to forbid every kind of cruelty towards animals, whether by way of amusement, or to gratify gluttony. Cock-fights, bull-baiting, hunting hares and foxes, fishing, and other amusements of the same kind, necessarily suppose either the absence of reflection or a fund of inhumanity, since they produce the most acute sufferings to sensible beings, and the most painful and lingering death of which we can form any idea. Why should the law refuse its protection to any sensitive being? The time will come when humanity will extend its mantle over everything which breathes. We have begun by attending to the condition of slaves; we shall finish by softening that of all the animals which assist our labours or supply our wants. . . .

Recognizing Animal Rights

For the present, however, what is most urgently needed is some comprehensive and intelligible principle, which shall indicate, in a more consistent manner, the true lines of man's moral relation towards the lower animals. And here, it must be admitted, our position is still far from satisfactory; for though certain very important concessions have been made, as we have seen, to the demand for the *jus an-*

imalium [justice for animals], they have been made for the most part in a grudging, unwilling spirit, and rather in the interests of *property* than of *principle;* while even the leading advocates of animals' rights seem to have shrunk from basing their claim on the only argument which can ultimately be held to be a really sufficient one—the assertion that animals, as well as men, though, of course, to a far less extent than men, are possessed of a distinctive individuality, and, therefore, are in justice entitled to live their lives with a due measure of that "restricted freedom" to which Herbert Spencer alludes. . . .

If we are ever going to do justice to the lower races, we must get rid of the antiquated notion of a "great gulf" fixed between them and mankind, and must recognize the common bond of humanity that unites all living beings in one universal brotherhood.

As far as any excuses can be alleged, in explanation of the insensibility or inhumanity of the western nations in their treatment of animals, these excuses may be mostly traced back to one or the other of two theoretical contentions, wholly different in origin, yet alike in this—that both postulate an absolute difference of nature between men and the lower kinds.

Religious Reasons

The first is the so-called "religious" notion, which awards immortality to man, but to man alone, thereby furnishing (especially in Catholic countries) a quibbling justification for acts of cruelty to animals, on the plea that they "have no souls." "It should seem," says a modern writer [Anna Jameson],

> as if the primitive Christians, by laying so much stress upon a future life, in contradistinction to *this* life, and placing the lower creatures out of the pale of hope, placed them at the same time out of the pale of sympathy, and thus laid the foundation for this utter disregard of animals in the light of our fellow-creatures.

I am aware that a quite contrary argument has, in a few isolated instances, been founded on the belief that animals have "no souls." Humphry Primatt, for example, says that "cruelty to a brute is an injury irreparable," because there is no future life to be a compensation for present afflictions; and there is an amusing story, told by [William] Lecky in his "History of European Morals," of a certain humanely-minded Cardinal, who used to allow vermin to bite him without hindrance, on the ground that "*we* shall have heaven to reward us for our sufferings, but these poor creatures have nothing but the enjoyment of this present life." But this is a rare view of the question which need not, I think, be taken into very serious account; for, on the whole, the denial of immortality to animals (unless, of course, it be also denied to men) tends strongly to lessen their chance of being justly and considerately treated. Among the many humane movements of the present age, none is more significant than the growing inclination, noticeable both in scientific circles and in religious, to believe that mankind and the lower animals have the same destiny before them, whether that destiny be for immortality or for annihilation.

Denying That Animals Feel

The second and not less fruitful source of modern inhumanity is to be found in the "Cartesian" doctrine—the theory of Descartes and his followers—that the lower animals are devoid of consciousness and feeling; a theory which carried the "religious" notion a step further, and deprived the animals not only of their claim to a life hereafter, but of anything that could, without mockery, be called a life in the present, since mere "animated machines," as they were thus affirmed to be, could in no real sense be said to *live* at all! Well might Voltaire turn his humane ridicule against this most monstrous contention, and suggest, with scathing irony, that God "had given the animals the organs of feeling, to the end that they might *not* feel!" "The theory of animal automatism," says one of the leading scientists of the present day [George Romanes], "which is usually attributed to Descartes, can never be accepted by common sense." Yet it is to be feared that it has done much, in its time, to harden "scientific" sense against the just complaints of the victims of human arrogance and oppression. . . .

To live one's own life—to realize one's true self—is the highest moral purpose of man and animal alike; and that animals possess their due measure of this sense of individuality is scarcely open to doubt. "We have seen," says Darwin,

> "that the senses and intuitions, the various emotions and faculties, such as love, memory, attention, curiosity, imitation, reason, etc., of which man boasts, may be found in an incipient, or even sometimes in a well-developed condition, in the lower animals.

Not less emphatic is the testimony of the Rev. J.G. Wood, who, speaking from a great experience, gives it as his opinion that "the manner in which we ignore individuality in the lower animals is simply astounding." He claims for them a future life, because he is "quite sure that most of the cruelties which are perpetrated on the animals are due to the habit of considering them as mere machines without susceptibilities, without reason, and without the capacity of a future."

This, then, is the position of those who assert that animals, like men, are necessarily possessed of certain limited rights, which cannot be withheld from them as they are now withheld without tyranny and injustice. They have individuality, character, reason; and to have those qualities is to have the right to exercise them, in so far as surrounding circumstances permit. "Freedom of choice and act," says Ouida [Marie Loise de la Ramée],

> is the first condition of animal as of human happiness. How many animals in a million have even relative freedom in any moment of their lives? No choice is ever permitted to them, and all their most natural instincts are denied or made subject to authority.

Yet no human being is justified in regarding any animal whatsoever as a meaningless automaton, to be worked, or tortured, or eaten, as the case may be, for the mere object of satisfying the wants or whims of mankind. Together with the destinies and duties that are laid on them and fulfilled by them, animals have also the right to be treated with gentleness and consideration, and the man who does not so treat them, however great his learning or influence may be, is, in that respect, an ignorant and foolish man, devoid of the highest and noblest culture of which the human mind is capable. . . .

Our main principle is now clear. If "rights" exist at all—and both feeling and usage indubitably prove that they do exist—they cannot be consistently awarded to men and denied to animals, since the same sense of justice and compassion apply in both cases. "Pain is pain," says an honest old writer [Humpry Primatt], "whether it be inflicted on man or on beast; and the creature that suffers it, whether man or beast, being sensible of the misery of it while it lasts, suffers *evil;* and the sufferance of evil, unmeritedly, unprovokedly, where no offence has been given, and no good can possibly be answered by it, but merely to exhibit power or gratify malice, is Cruelty and Injustice in him that occasions it."

Animal Experimentation Is Cruel to Animals and to Human Beings

ENID WIDDRINGTON

The following piece, which explains the motivations and aims of the antivivisection movement, is an excerpt from an address delivered in 1903 to the American Anti-Vivisection Society by Enid Widdrington, an English activist. According to Widdrington, those opposed to vivisection, or animal experimentation, are not opposed to the killing of animals but rather to the infliction of pain and suffering. She argues that it is absurd to suppose, as some scientists did, that such animals as dogs, cats, and horses do not feel pain when they are experimented upon. Furthermore, she points out, if it were true that animals do not have the capacity to feel pain, then this would suggest their physiology is very different from human physiology, which would tend to undermine the supposed benefits to humans of animal research. Finally, Widdrington argues that human excellence consists not in bodily health and longevity but in mental and moral superiority. Experimenting on animals, she believes, may help human beings live longer or healthier lives, but it requires that we abandon the human qualities of love, mercy, sympathy, and compassion by which our lives should be judged.

Enid Widdrington, address before the American Anti-Vivisection Society, Philadelphia, PA, January 29, 1903.

Of course, in what I am going to say to-night I am not taking the extremely narrow and illogical position of objecting to vivisection whilst calmly tolerating many other forms of cruelty to animals and living creatures. It is sometimes urged against the anti-vivisectionists—however, I think unfairly—that they are so taken up with their particular hobby of the stopping of scientific research as regards the work upon animals that they are tending to strain at a gnat and swallow a camel, because of the immense amount of cruelty that is perpetrated on the animal world elsewhere. Now, I believe that this criticism is undeserved. Anti-vivisection is a part of a movement which is a part of a bigger movement; it is part of that bigger movement directed against the infliction of wanton and unnecessary cruelty and torture upon the animal world. We oppose cruelty and vivisection wherever we find them. . . . What do we mean by vivisection? Of course we do not mean taking the animal's life for the purpose of science, for the purpose of clothing, or for anything else. It is not the taking of life that constitutes vivisection; it is torture and torment and the inflicting of terrible agony upon the animals while they are living. It is not death we are opposed to, but torture. Although I do not wish for one moment to harrow you with any of the terrible details of these operations, it is well that we should bear in mind that there are no forms of torture but what are committed in the name of vivisection. All kinds of horrors have been and are being perpetrated on helpless animals in the name of science; not upon the animals low down, about whose powers or sense of feeling there may be some doubt, but animals as high in the scale of human feeling as the horse, the cat, and the dog—warm-blooded animals, whose systems more nearly approach ours. These animals have been and are being subjected all over this land, and in all other civilized countries, to the most agonizing cruelties; cut up and left to die; burned slowly to death; covered with paraffin and set a light to; torn to pieces, their nerves exposed, and then an electric battery applied to them. There is, in fact, no kind of horror that has not been committed in the name of science. It is not for me to outline the character of these barbarities any further, because, if you so desire, there are plenty of means open to you whereby you can only too sadly find out for yourselves how true my words are and how difficult it is to give any real idea of them in an address, because it would be too horrible for a speaker to be able to handle at all. But when you read the life of Claude Bernard, the Prince of Vivisectors, in which he describes the various operations, we can appreciate their horrors; when we read the book written by the Italian, Mantegazza, in which he says that he tried to find out how much pain—"shock," he called it—the animal could stand without dying. When we read these books, it seems almost impossible to credit [believe] them; but then these are the experiments written down by the experimenters themselves; they are not charges made against them by persons who had merely witnessed these operations. We are made fully to believe them as an account of the experimenters themselves, and we are obliged to believe their terrible accounts of pain inflicted upon the helpless animals. The very looking at these things shocks the conscience of decent people. It is so terrible that people will not believe that these things do happen, except when they are plainly proved to them.

Denying Animals Feel Pain

The first question is, How is it that such a practice is tolerated for one hour, for one day, in a civilized country, especially in ours, which prides itself on being humane? I am not sure that there are not signs that the humanity of the twentieth century has undergone a sad reaction, as contrasted with that of the nineteenth century. The first plea that is made for vivisection is an extraordinary one. It is that the animals do not suffer. The first way in which this plea is put is that the animals' nervous systems, their powers of sensation, are so utterly unlike ours that you cannot make any kind of comparison. It is absurd to think, because the animal writhes, and moans, and twists, and turns, and makes all the signs that a human being does when suffering—it is absurd, say the vivisectors, to say that this animal feels anything we do; and then they talk learnedly about reflex action, etc. I am not here to argue whether this is or is not the case; I only ask, if it be true that these animals are so entirely different that they do not feel anything like the way we do, of what possible use are the experiments? What is their object? How can they have any kind of effect upon life, if the animal really is so entirely unlike the human being as regards its physical make-up? (Applause.) How utterly unwise and unsafe it would be for them to argue from what has been done to an animal, what can be done to a human being, suffering from what seemed to be the same disease! If this were true, it would absolutely destroy the theory of the vivisectors that the experiments are performed for the benefit they exert upon human life. But, says the vivisector, we do not mean that they do not feel pain at all; we mean that they do not feel a great deal of pain; we do not allow them to suffer, because all our experiments are performed under an anaesthetic. . . .

But by far the greater bulk of the operations are not performed by the aid of any anaesthetic at all. . . .

With this anti-vivisection law in England, last year, out of the 8000 operations of this kind done in that country, over 7000 were not done under anaesthesia. In many of the operations performed, the animals were allowed to recover from the anaesthesia so that they might be studied for several days, or weeks, or months, as long as their lives and sufferings lasted. This large proportion is done without anaesthetics, that these vivisectors might observe the influence of the operation on the animal. And the majority of these, they claim, are not operations at all. . . .

They consist in inserting the initial germ of a painful, lingering disease, such as small-pox, typhoid fever, or hydrophobia. The operation itself, of course, is not so very difficult or painful, but it may be far more terrible than an agonizing operation which lasts for an hour or so, because the animals, after undergoing it, live a painful existence for days, weeks, or in some cases even months, and at last die wretchedly and in the height of misery. . . .

A Selfish Principle

From this it is quite plain that the animals do suffer; that they are not by any means in every case, or even as a general rule, under the influence of an anaesthetic; and that even when an anaesthetic is administered during the primary operation, they are allowed to recover from its effects in order to study their condition. This is done every day, and the growing prevalence is remarkable of these injections of disease into animals by the tens of thousands,—yes, I may say hundreds of thousands,—from frogs up to horses, cats, and dogs, which, of course, in every case means days and weeks of pain and wretchedness, before death finally relieves the disease-stricken creature. The first plea is that the practice of vivisection is justifiable in order to cure human ills. Now observe first of all the rank selfishness of that plea. You are urged, when your nature revolts against these cruelties, to put up with them and approve of them, in the hope that some day you individually may be cured of a disease that you may suffer from, by means of these experiments. Of course, that is what every plea must come down to. It comes down to human safety, and perchance it may come down to individual safety. It is admittedly an absolutely selfish principle. Torture animals in the hope that some day you, as an individual, will gain safety from it! . . .

Human Superiority

Now I come to the real crux of the whole matter. Let us grant, for the sake of argument, that it is possible by these methods to devise cures for all varieties of human ills; grant that we have such a knowledge of anatomy that will enable us to understand the cure of certain diseases; grant that we can preserve for a certain length of time human life beyond the natural period; yet I would say frankly, in spite of all that, that if all the claims made in this behalf are true claims, then I have only to say that I would oppose vivisection just as strenuously as I do now; because, if you will go carefully into the question, you will find that those men who are most interested in vivisection are not those who are chiefly interested in this humane plea at all; many of them never went to a university at all. But what are they interested in? The answer is, pure research for the love of research. They say science for science's sake. I do not believe in science for science's sake any more than I believe in art for art's sake. To me humanity is, after all, the test of all things which affect human people. But just because I do believe in the supremacy of humanity in this wise, I cannot tolerate the infliction of torture upon animals for the sole purpose of insuring the health of our bodily frames. Because wherein does this supremacy consist? It consists not in the superiority of our bodily forms, for they are of little or no superior physical excellence to some animals. But the superiority is in our mental and our moral faculties— our superior nature. It is in these directions that we claim human superiority. Now, if the endeavor to live a few years longer has been our object, we are falling to the lowest depths of our moral and our mental nature; we are destroying our human supremacy; we are absolutely placing our lives merely upon a level with the animal world, because in order to add a few more years to our existence we are inflicting torture upon animals who cannot speak. To tolerate and approve of these operations, because of the good they can get to their bodies through such practices, would be one of the most pitiable of human attributes. But this plea which is so frequently offered, is one of the most dangerous pleas that can be brought forward. The plea of science for science's sake is of no more weight than the plea of commerce for commerce's sake, or the plea of art for art's sake; and in those countries where they believe in commerce for commerce's sake, where their entire time is devoted to studying the tables of their export and their import trade, we find slight regard for the quality of humanity. If they are working for commerce for commerce's sake, they have no regard as to whether that commerce is ruining human nature.

It is exactly the same thing in science. Where science is followed for science's sake, the people are not living out and observing those principles which are most beautiful and perfect in humanity. What is most beautiful in humanity? The qualities of purity, virtue, and justice; the qualities of love, mercy, sympathy, and compassion, and those who have those qualities are high up in the scale of being. But it is not beautiful to approve of the principles of vivisection and subject helpless animals to torture for the sake of relieving ourselves of pain, or perhaps adding a few years to our existence. It is not just to treat these creatures who cannot protest, who have no voice, in this manner. These animals have a right to human sympathy, and it is cruel to subject them to these tortures. It is cruel to the animals and it is more cruel to ourselves, because it lowers us further in the scale of being, than the animals we have tortured, for in this practice of vivisection we are certainly below the animals. We do sink below the animals when, in order to lengthen out by a few years our existence in this world, we inflict these tortures. It would be very little good to humanity to increase the length of our physical life, granting that it could be done by the discoveries brought about by vivisection, if, while increasing the quantity of our lives, we were decreasing and vitiating its quality; if, while we lengthened out our miserable lives in this world, we had rendered ourselves absolutely unfitted for a life of blessedness in the world to come.

The Rise of Legal Protection for Animals

ROSWELL McCREA

The following selection is from The Humane Movement,
*Roswell McCrea's 1910 history of the early animal rights
movement. In the excerpt, McCrea notes that the movement
began in England early in the nineteenth century and soon
spread to other Commonwealth countries and the United
States. McCrea traces the development of anticruelty laws in
England and in the United States, pointing out that by 1910
every state had implemented some kind of anticruelty statute.
According to McCrea, although most states had a general law
against cruelty to animals, this was usually supplemented
with more detailed laws that restricted specific activities, such
as the fighting or baiting of animals, the use of dogs as draft
animals, animal experimentation, neglect, and the inhumane
transportation and disposal of animals. Furthermore, he says,
most states began to incorporate lessons on the humane treatment of animals into school curricula.*

L ess than a century ago (1811) Lord Erskine stood up in
the British House of Lords to ask for justice to the
lower creatures. At that time there was practically no law
for the protection of animals, and no machinery for enforcing any law that might have been on the statute books.
The mocking treatment of Lord Erskine when he made his

Roswell McCrea, *The Humane Movement: A Descriptive Survey.* New York: Columbia University Press, 1910.

plea for mercy, and the open derision of his argument in favor of the rights of animals to humane treatment are a fitting index of the prevailing indifference of the period. Ignorance, heedlessness, and wanton brutality contributed to a situation that caused much animal suffering, and the few who openly protested against this cruelty were regarded with scorn and indignation. Among the working classes there was open disregard of the bodily sufferings of cattle and of draught animals on highways and streets; and among the wealthier, as well as with the poorer classes, cruel sports were very common.

The first legislative dealings with this situation were in 1822, when Parliament passed "An Act to Prevent the Cruel and Improper Treatment of Cattle" introduced by Richard Martin, an Irish member. Two years later the founding of the Society for the Prevention of Cruelty to Animals provided by delegated authority the machinery for enforcing the new law. But the Society and the country (*i.e.*, the wealthier class, for at that time the working classes did not count politically) were caught in a dilemma: how to protect the horse and other cattle without checking the sportsman. Martin's Act had excluded the protection of the bull and the dog from its provisions. This suited the temper of the country, but was obnoxious to the founders of the Society. They accordingly put in the front of the Society's program the obtaining of amendments to the law of 1822. These were secured in 1835. The bull, dog and lamb were now recognized as "cattle," and the baiting or fighting of dogs, bulls, bears, badgers and cocks was prohibited. In 1845 there followed an amendment of the law for regulating Knockers' Yards [slaughter house]; in 1849 a new and much improved Act for the more effectual Prevention of Cruelty to Animals; in 1854 an Act prohibiting the use of dogs as beasts of draught or burden throughout England; and numerous more recent acts covering among other things, the following objects: for the regulation of experiments on live animals; for insuring for animals carried by sea (both foreign and domestic) a proper supply of food and water and proper ventilation during the passage and on landing; for protecting them from unnecessary suffering during passage and on landing and during inland transit; for regulating the marking of animals; for regulating the conduct of slaughter houses; for the placing of poisonous matter in open places; and for the protection of wild birds. There has been a constant expansion of the sphere of animal protection, until with the enactment of 63-4 Vic. c. 33 (1900) wild animals were included. The Act was then made to apply to all animals in captivity, but not under all circumstances. It did not apply to animals being killed for food, nor to those vivisected under the terms of the Act of 1876, nor to tame animals turned out to be coursed or hunted, unless they had previously been mutilated to facilitate their recapture. There has since been considerable effort still further to extend the application of the law; but no vital amendments have been made. Particularly in the matter of the law covering vivisection, the pressure has been very strong. Very detailed evidence was gathered by the Royal Commission on Vivisection during 1907, and presented to Parliament. But the status of the law has not been changed.

An Idea Spreads

Similar laws have been adopted from time to time, largely as the outcome of the activity of societies for the prevention of cruelty, in Germany, France, and other European countries. In the British colonies the English example has been closely followed in most instances, particularly in Canada and the Australasian states; and protective laws exist and are more or less vigorously enforced in the more important South American countries.

In the United States, there were protective laws on the statute books of certain states before Henry Bergh began his campaign of animal protection. Noteworthy among these was the following Pennsylvania law of March 31, 1860: "If any person shall wantonly and cruelly beat, torture, kill, or maim any horse or other domestic animal, whether belonging to himself or another, every such person so offending shall be guilty of a misdemeanor, and on conviction, be sentenced to pay a fine not exceeding two hundred dollars, or undergo an imprisonment not exceeding one year, or both, or either at the discretion of the Court."

But the first effective piece of legislation in this direction, accompanied by sincere and adequate machinery of enforcement, was the New York law of April 19, 1866, passed nine days after the incorporation of the American Society for the Prevention of Cruelty to Animals. Similar laws were soon passed in the following few years in New Jersey, Pennsylvania, Massachusetts and in other New England, middle, and middle-western states. Other states have since followed, details of legislation have been refined and amplified, until today there is not a state nor territory without some statutory provision for animal protection.

Protecting Animals

Proceeding to a more detailed description of State laws, the most common provision is that which provides against the overloading, over-driving, unnecessary or unjustifiable beating, killing, mutilating or maiming of animals, and the failure to provide necessary and proper food, drink and shelter, and against any other act of cruelty to an animal. The New York law is representative in this connection: "A person who overdrives, overloads, tortures, or cruelly beats or unjustifiably injures, maims, mutilates, or kills any animal, whether wild or tame, and whether belonging to himself or to another, or deprives any animal of necessary sustenance, food or drink, or neglects or refuses to furnish it such sustenance or drink, or causes, procures, or permits any animal to be overdriven, overloaded, tortured, cruelly beaten, or unjustifiably injured, maimed, mutilated, or killed, or to be deprived of necessary food or drink, or who wilfully sets on foot, instigates, engages in, or in any way furthers an act of cruelty to any animal, or any act tending to produce such cruelty, is guilty of a misdemeanor.". . .

The fighting or baiting of animals obviously comes within the general statutory prohibition of wanton cruelty. Yet the majority of the states have passed specific laws against the practice. These usually include in the category of offenders not merely the immediate promoters of fights, but also the trainers and owners of fighting animals and paraphernalia, owners and lessors of premises used for fights, and spectators. Fighting animals and accessory property are usually seized, whether the laws specifically provide to that effect or not. . . .

Many minor offenses require no such administrative detail. In consequence, they are usually left uncovered by law, except by the general enactment. The use of dogs as draft animals is a good example of this. Only two states have specific enactments covering this matter. It is, of course, almost a negligible practice at any rate. The New York law, assuming that under proper supervision the use of dogs in this way is not necessarily cruel, specifically permits the practice on taking out a license the number of which must be painted on any vehicle drawn by dogs. The New Jersey law, on the other hand, summarily forbids the practice, and provides that any cart so attached shall, with its contents, be subject to seizure. The other states recognize the matter only as they would in the case of a horse, mule, or other large draft animal, overloaded or maltreated.

Restricting Animal Experimentation

The use of live animals for purposes of scientific experimentation has been treated in like fashion. Except where specific exception has been made, the general anti-cruelty law covers abuses involving cruelty to vivisected animals. It is usually assumed, however, that experiments conducted under the authority of a regular medical school or college are so carried on as to avoid unnecessary suffering. Such institutions are therefore largely immune from interference in this connection. Isolated instances of vivisection under private auspices are those in which abuses are most likely to occur. Against these the general law very well applies. This being the case, several states have taken the step of permitting such experiments "only under the authority of the faculty of some regularly incorporated medical college or university of the state" in question. In Illinois, Massachusetts, Oklahoma, Pennsylvania and Washington, vivisection, as well as the exhibition of vivisected animals, is forbidden in schools, other than medical and dental. The most restrictive of any of the state laws is probably that of Michigan, passed in 1907. This law specifies a considerable list of experiments, presumably of more or less serious or painful type, all of which are forbidden except under anaesthetics. The English law is more detailed and more restrictive in its provisions than any of these. Its administration is such, however, that effective supervision is a matter of difficulty. . . . .

The Cruelty of Neglect

Aside from the general provision against cruelty, none is more common in the laws of the states than those providing against neglect in its various forms. Failure to provide proper food, drink and protection against the weather for domestic animals is a misdemeanor in most of the states. In nearly one half of these the law is worked out in sufficient detail not merely to prescribe proper penalties for offenders, but to suggest as well lawful methods of relieving the distress of another's neglected beast. It is provided in these cases that after the lapse of a reasonable time (usually twelve successive hours) an outsider may make necessary provision for a neglected animal. It is lawful for such person to enter another's premises from time to time with this end in view without incurring liability to any action for such entry. The reasonable expense of food and water so provided is chargeable to the offending owner of such an animal. In default of payment, the animal is subject to levy and sale upon observance of usual legal processes. . . .

Humane Transportation and Disposal

In the carrying of animals, whether locally or over long distances, laws for the protection of live-stock have had considerable development along specific lines. The general statute would obviously apply here without further specification. But the difficulties of the case are such that definite requirements have proved to be a necessity. In the first place, the commercial incentive is so largely involved that in many instances of treatment producing baneful effects on animals, the question of intent is very much obscured by other considerations. There is a seeming economy in overcrowding and in a minimum of care during transportation, in which it is difficult to find any element of wanton cruelty. Then too, especially in railroad transportation, the field for discretion in determining proper standards is so broad that adequate restrictions can be provided only by specific statutory enactments of a rather detailed type. . . .

In the matter of diseased, disabled or superannuated animals statutory enactments are numerous. Abandonment of animals past useful service is forbidden with particular frequency. In some states, abandonment is simply forbidden under penalty. No further provision is made in these states covering the disposition of abandoned animals. More frequently, however, there is additional stipulation that such animals shall be humanely killed. To guard against possibly unjust or hasty destruction of property in this way, simple judicial machinery is usually provided for by the law, to pass on the question of killing an abandoned animal. In Delaware, for instance, a justice of the peace must order the killing and removal of such an animal. This act is almost invariably performed by a police officer or the agent of a local humane society. . . .

Educating Americans About Animal Welfare

By way of furthering humane education, state legislation has done little beyond recognizing humane societies,

Audubon societies and other organizations as agencies for its promotion. A succession of New York laws provide for an agreement with the American Museum of Natural History in New York City by the terms of which materials, specimens, etc., are provided for free instruction in natural history in normal and other schools for the preparation of teachers, and in free common schools. Further lectures are also provided for, to be given on holidays and at other suitable times to artisans, mechanics and other citizens. In Illinois, California and some other states the law provides for an annual "Bird Day" in the schools. The law of Colorado requires that two lessons per week (not less than ten minutes each) be given in the schools on the humane treatment of animals. The law of North Dakota prescribes a like period for "a system of study of the humane treatment of animals," as do the laws of South Dakota, Montana and Wyoming. The latter three, however, specify "a system of humane treatment as embodied in the laws" of the respective states, and do not prescribe a definite period of instruction. In California, humane education is compulsory in all primary and grammar schools having more than one hundred census children in the district. This instruction may be oral, and the purchase of text-books may not be required of pupils. In Oklahoma the law prescribes instruction in schools to the amount of not less than one-half hour per week on the "humane treatment and protection of dumb animals and birds; their lives, habits and usefulness, and the important part they are intended to fulfill in the economy of nature." The Illinois law is similar; but is more extended. The Pennsylvania law provides for not more than one-half hour per week on the "kind treatment of birds and animals," and those of Maine and Washington for not less than ten minutes. The law of Texas prescribes that "suitable instruction shall be given in the primary grades once each week regarding kindness to animals of the brute creation and the protection of birds and their nests and eggs." The New Hampshire statute provides for "a well prescribed reading course dealing with the principle of the humane treatment of the lower animals." Idaho and Utah have been reported as having compulsory requirements; but I have been unable to find any specific enactments to that effect. . . .

Viewing the field of legislation as a whole, it will be seen that there is no state nor territory lacking some general provision under which cruelty to animals may be prosecuted and punished. In most of the states the law has undergone considerable differentiation in detail; and in such states as California, Colorado, Massachusetts and others, the law leaves little to be desired on the score of completeness. It is unquestionably true that the degree of detail with which the law of any state has been worked out is a fairly satisfactory index of the past activity of its humane organizations.

Experiments on Animals Are Justified

WALTER BRADFORD CANNON

In the following excerpt from his 1945 memoir, Walter Bradford Cannon argues that the antivivisection movement of the early twentieth century was a dangerous and misguided threat to scientific discovery. According to Cannon, those who opposed vivisection, or animal experimentation, were quite mistaken in alleging that it usually involves inflicting pain on animals. To the contrary, Cannon says, most experiments are done with anesthetic and animals show little discomfort during postoperative recovery. Furthermore, Cannon says, the benefits of animal experimentation—to humans and to other animals—far outweigh whatever harm is done to animals through the experiments. Cannon recounts how, as the head of a group of scientists opposed to laws banning animal experimentation, he helped institute voluntary standards for humane treatment of animals and to educate the public about the benefits of using animals for research.

Investigators who employ living animals for experimental purposes not only confront more complex problems than do the physicists and the chemists but they also confront a hostile group of zealous opponents. These are the fighting antivivisectionists—of whom I shall have more to say later—the success of whose efforts would interfere with

---

Walter Bradford Cannon, *The Way of an Investigator: A Scientist's Experiences in Medical Research*. New York: W.W. Norton & Co., 1945.

the activities of the investigators and might even abolish the means through which their experimental work can arrive at its beneficent consequences. The word "vivisection" is unfortunate because it has various meanings which are not clearly distinguished. To the antivivisectionists the word too frequently signifies the cutting or dissection of sentient living animals, bound or otherwise restrained and without anesthesia subjected to the full torture of extensive operations. The repeated tales of assumed cruelty, the unexplained illustrations of instruments used in laboratory procedures, and the imaginary pictures of sufferings the animals are supposed to endure at the hands of experimenters indicate the hideous significance attached by the zealots to the word "vivisection."

To the medical investigator, on the contrary, the word has a quite different significance. It means, to be sure, operations on living animals but it does not imply attendant pain, any more than does an operation on a living man by a surgeon. And if an animal is anesthetized, then operated upon, and is killed without recovery from anesthesia, clearly the procedure has not involved any pain whatever. The operation would not have been different in effect, so far as the experience of the animal is concerned, if it had first been killed and later dissected. There is abundant evidence that in almost all physiological experiments the observations on living processes are made in precisely this way, i.e., while the animals are on the way to painless death by anesthesia. In medical investigations substances are injected and sometimes diseases are produced; and in surgical research it is occasionally necessary, after a painless operation, to keep the animals alive in order to observe the effects of the procedure. In these instances of inoculation and aseptic operation, the animals may feel ill, as they would with a distemper. The pain of inoculation is trifling; and in the vast majority of operations even on human beings the aseptic healing of wounds, as I can testify from personal experience, causes no considerable discomfort after full recovery from the anesthetic. Were lower animals as sensitive as man, therefore, the pain would not be great, and there are good indications that they are not as sensitive. The sight of an animal contentedly munching its food a short time after an operation is commonplace in laboratory experience. The total amount of pain resulting from animal experimentation is in all antivivisection literature grossly exaggerated.

Misleading Claims

Yet the testimony that the immense majority of operations in experimental medicine are attended by little or no suffering is everywhere opposed by the antivivisectionists in their writings. Some of the reports they cite are based on experiments performed more than a century ago, before the discovery of anesthesia; some are frankly of the class of experiments involving slight pain and discomfort; some are clear instances of misrepresentation by persons too unfamiliar with bodily functions and the effects of anesthetic agents to understand ordinary biological description. Many decades since, my teacher of physiology, Dr. H.P. Bowditch, in testing whether a nerve could be fatigued, cut the nerve while the animal was completely under the effects of ether and then stimulated the isolated end. Commenting on this experiment, a representative of the New England Antivivisection Society declared, "It will be readily seen, even by the casual reader, that it involves an amount of agony beyond which science is unable to go and which, to approximate, is impossible except by a person who has devoted long years to the study of nerves." Despite clear explanation that not even trivial pain could be inflicted by stimulating a piece of nerve quite separated from the brain, the society continued for nearly a human generation to broadcast this ancient slander.

More recent studies carried on by me or under my direction have not escaped denunciation by the antivivisectionists. An operative procedure was performed on cats under scrupulously considerate surgical precautions, in order to avoid both pain and infection, and aftercare was provided which included warmth and a comfortable resting place. Within half a day the animals were up and moving about and took their food as usual the next morning; thereafter they wandered about the laboratory, rubbing their sides against table legs or coming to be petted, and exhibited no signs of discomfort. Yet in an antivivisection periodical they were described as "wretched animals," which had undergone a "frightful operation" and were subjected to "exquisitely contrived torture," suffering "agonies not to be described." Such perverse charges made by persons who did not see what they described are fair illustrations of the sort of criticism to which medical investigators may be subjected. I was once informed: "Such men as you ought to be tarred and feathered and I would like to help do it, too."

Interfering with Science

While his conscience is quite clear, the "vivisector" is not likely to enjoy being reviled and hearing all manner of evil said against him falsely. Still more unfavorable to his work, however, is the continuous agitation for passage of hostile laws that would restrict freedom of medical research. Commonly, every winter when legislatures meet, there are introduced, now in one state now in another, bills directed toward that dangerous purpose. These efforts, unfortunately, must be met by some of the "vivisectors" themselves. They act for the public to protect from ruthless interference a method of investigation which has done more for mankind, by bringing release from devastating diseases and from premature death, than any other human endeavor. To protect it, however, takes valuable time. . . .

When I was a medical student I heard a talk by the late William T. Sedgwick, in which he advised his listeners first to establish themselves in their professional careers, perhaps by the time they reached forty years of age, and thereafter to spend weekly a certain amount of time in attention to public affairs. This talk made a deep impression. Not until I was nearly forty years old did the chance come for me to follow Professor Sedgwick's suggestion. In 1908 I was chairman of the Section on Physiology and Pathology of the American Medical Association. For more than a decade the antivivisectionists had striven to restrict freedom of medical research in Massachusetts, and during about the same period they had made similar efforts in Pennsylvania. It seemed to me pertinent to discuss the aims of the antivivisectionists, their misconceptions, the methods they employed to realize their objectives, and the danger which might ensue to the population at large, should they be successful. This I did in my chairman's address.

The fundamental mischief of the antivivisectionists in agitating against medical research is, as I have already pointed out, their presentation of a misleading issue. They deny that any utility has come from animal experimentation, they describe the experiments as horrible torturing of dumb brutes, and then they ask if this futile cruelty shall be permitted to go on. If this were the whole and veracious story, few would hesitate on which side to stand. Every decent man and woman is opposed to cruelty; every decent human being winces at the thought of inflicted pain. But that is not the whole story. Nor is it veracious. It would be as fair to display a picture of Dr. Grenfell, fighting his faithful dogs and stabbing them to death, labeled "Is this the way to treat your pets?" as it is to represent animal experimentation without its motives and without its triumphs. Grenfell, in his struggle on the frigid ice pan, stabbed his dogs in order to save his own life, and every person with common sense commends the bravery, the resourcefulness, and the proper sense of values of that missionary hero. Any worthy man who sees straight would try to do what Grenfell did, if he were cornered and had to sacrifice his own life or that of lower animals.

This is precisely the issue which the investigators see. Furthermore, they are aware of overwhelming evidence that by the experimental use of some animals the chances for life and health of all mankind, and of myriads of lower animals as well, have been enormously amplified. All that the uninstructed need do is to read what is known regarding the direct and practical relation of animal experiments to the effective treatment of diphtheria and tetanus, to meningitis, rabies, and smallpox to dysentery, cholera and typhoid fever, to bubonic plague, tuberculosis and syphilis, to the disturbances of internal secretions, to diabetes and pernicious anemia, to the action of drugs, to the advancement of surgical technique, to childbirth, to hygiene and preventive medicine—in order to learn of the incomparable service which animals in the laboratories have rendered for their fellow creatures. Just because they have rendered such service, we turn to them for succor as we contemplate the still unconquered afflictions of men and women and children whose sufferings extend to everyone bound to them by the strong ties of love and sympathy. Of the animal used for solving the mystery of disease William James wrote, with illuminating insight, "If his poor benighted mind could only be made to catch a glimpse of the human intentions, all that is heroic in him would religiously acquiesce."

Such points as these I emphasized in my address. In the audience was the eminent pathologist, William H. Welch, who, at a famous hearing before a Congressional Committee in Washington in 1900, had proved himself a vigorous defender of freedom of medical investigation. Whether in consequence of the address I do not know, but almost immediately thereafter the Association appointed a Committee for the Protection of Medical Research, and asked me to be chairman. . . .

Setting Up Rules

This group, with few changes, worked together for seventeen years. Our first task was to examine the conditions under which experimental medicine was being conducted in the United States. Inquiry revealed that in a number of laboratories there had been posted for many years regulations defining the humane treatment of animals used for experimental purposes. We collected these scattered regulations and generalized them so that they would be applicable throughout the country. They provided for caution in using stray cats and dogs by arranging a delay before their use, at least as long as that which was customary in the local pound; they stipulated the kind of care in the housing and feeding of the animals; they demanded use of anesthesia when the operative procedure involved more discomfort than that of giving the anesthetic; and they provided for putting the animals to death before recovery from the anesthetic unless the director of the laboratory authorized recovery for the purposes of the experiment. These regulations were printed on a large display card. They were adopted by corporate action of medical faculties and medical research institutes throughout the United States, and the cards were prominently posted in laboratory rooms wherever experimental work was being carried on. The members of the Committee were convinced that these regulations were chiefly valuable in assuring the interested public that the procedures in animal experimentation are conducted in a humane manner.

As intimated above, antivivisection literature reveals the prevalence of two general ideas. First, there is the charge that animals are experimented on with utter disregard for avoidance of inflicting pain; indeed, many of the claims of cruelty in medical research would give the uninstructed reader the impression that the experimenters are hideous, immoral monsters. This is a view which might be corrected by actual visits to the laboratories. In 1923, the Committee was so thoroughly convinced that the methods of animal experimentation were routinely above reproach in the judgment of reasonable persons that it secured adherence from the deans of medical schools throughout the land to what was called the "open-door policy." This policy provided that any interested member of a humane society might visit the laboratories at any time. The only qualification imposed in some instances was that the visitor must previously have seen an operation on a human being. It is an instructive fact that very few representatives of humane societies have taken advantage of this opportunity.

Defending Vivisection

The Committee also met the second charge of the antivivisectionists—that animal experimentation is both misleading and useless. Even when the Committee was established, more than a third of a century ago, the charge had little force. Antiseptic surgery and aseptic surgery had become recognized as a consequence of experiments on lower animals, the death rate from diphtheria and tuberculosis had markedly dropped (in both diseases the result of animal experimentation), and other similar achievements could be pointed to with satisfaction. Nevertheless, there was no widespread understanding of the importance of the experimental method for the advancement of medical knowledge. In order to diffuse the evidence for that fact, well-known experts in various fields were invited to prepare articles on the vital significance of animal experiments for progress in practical medicine and surgery—articles on diphtheria, tuberculosis, child-bed fever, venereal disease, disorders of the heart and blood vessels, surgical technique, veterinary medicine, tropical disease, and other subjects. These authoritative expositions were published in the *Journal of the American Medical Association* and later reprinted as pamphlets. They had wide distribution and doubtless did much to acquaint both the profession and the public with the essential value of laboratory experimentation for the welfare of human beings and the welfare of lower animals also. In the last three decades the demonstration of these values has become so familiar to the public that the antivivisectionists' charge of uselessness is reduced to absurdity. Indeed, now that hundreds of thousands of Americans contribute to a fund, part of which is used to carry on animal experiments in order to secure insight into the nature of infantile paralysis, the antivivisectionists are having more and more difficulty in obtaining support for their harmful agitation.

In England where, since 1876, there has been restrictive legislation against the use of animals for medical and biological research, the antivivisection societies were not reduced in number thereby but in fact increased, until there were a dozen or more. Restrictive legislation is not sufficient for them; it is the camel's head inside the tent. The ultimate purpose of the extremist is not to restrict but to abolish the practice. It is immoral, they declare, to take the lives of lower animals as they are taken in the laboratories, even though mankind is benefited thereby—hence no compromise. We have been warned against following England's example and strongly advised against allowing even the initial steps of restrictive legislation. The Committee for the Protection of Medical Research has fought the efforts of the antivivisectionists to pass hostile bills in the legislatures of various eastern states, in Congress, and in popular referenda in Colorado and California. It is gratifying to report that thus far the antivivisectionists have not been able in the United States to interfere with medical investigators in their efforts to increase knowledge of disease and to discover effective ways of treating it. With due precautions against the infliction of pain they are still as free as the experimenters in physics and chemistry to project their explorations into the dark ranges of ignorance.

THE
HISTORY
OF
ISSUES

CHAPTER 2

Philosophical Debates over Animal Rights

A Moral Protest Is Born

JAMES M. JASPER AND DOROTHY NELKIN

In the following article, sociologists James M. Jasper and Dorothy Nelkin describe how the issue of animal rights grew out of the work of contemporary philosophers. According to Jasper and Nelkin, until the publication of Peter Singer's book Animal Liberation, *very few people were involved in the animal rights movement and it had little respectability. Singer argued, however, that animals have interests because they are able to feel pleasure and pain and that human beings ought to give the interests of animals equal consideration. His book also documented painful scientific experiments on animals and the harsh conditions farm animals endure. Jasper and Nelkin note that although Singer was the first modern voice to give animal rights activism an intellectual footing, his was soon supplemented by that of Tom Regan, another philosopher. Regan went beyond Singer, and argued in his 1984 text* The Case for Animal Rights *that animals had rights equal to those of humans. According to Regan, it is never acceptable to experiment on animals, no matter how great the benefits might be to human beings.*

A
s "professionals" of moral discourse, philosophers who deal with ethical questions have a natural—and central—role to play in moral crusades, and they were crucial to the birth of the animal rights movement. Just as philosophers, poets, and priests had questioned the treatment of

James M. Jasper and Dorothy Nelkin, *The Animal Rights Crusade: The Growth of a Moral Protest.* New York: The Free Press, 1992. Copyright © 1992 by James M. Jasper and Dorothy Nelkin. All rights reserved. Reproduced by permission of Simon & Schuster, Inc.

animals in the eighteenth century, so do many philosophers criticize the uses of animals today. But beyond their role as social critics, moral philosophers are attracted to this issue as a way to explore such fundamental philosophical questions as "What does it mean to be human?" and "What are the bases of moral rights?" Some debate these issues in the professional arena, but many philosophers have taken activist roles, developing moral arguments to generate political advocacy.

Philosophers served as midwives of the animal rights movement in the late 1970s. Through their prolific writing, they combined the emotional appeal of the humane and welfare traditions with the institutional critique of environmentalists. Through their ideas, the animal rights movement developed an agenda that won the hearts and the minds of people seeking ways to articulate their growing concern for animals. The moral sentiments were there; so were models of engaged activism; what was needed was an explicit ideology that could link feelings to actions on behalf of animals.

A Bible for the Movement

Almost every animal rights activist either owns or has read Peter Singer's *Animal Liberation*, which since its publication in 1975 has become a bible for the movement. Singer is an Australian philosopher committed to the analysis of moral disputes, and in the preface to his 1971 Oxford thesis, published as *Democracy and Disobedience*, Singer urged philosophers to leave their abstract word games and take stances on moral issues:

> If philosophers are to say anything of importance about major issues, they must go beyond the neutral analysis of words and concepts which was, until recently, characteristic of contemporary philosophy in Britain and America. Moral and political philosophers must be prepared to give their opinions, with supporting arguments, on the rights and wrongs of complex disputes.

This argument was a call to arms for his profession, heavily dominated at that time by an analytic tradition more concerned with clever language analyses than moral issues.

Singer grounded his argument about the treatment of animals in a utilitarian perspective. For utilitarians, ethical decisions should be made by adding up all pleasures and pains that would result from different choices, and choosing the option yielding the greatest aggregate pleasure (or happiness). Jeremy Bentham, founder of utilitarianism, had specifically applied his philosophy to animals in 1789: "The day *may* come when the rest of the animal creation may acquire those rights which never could have been withholden from them but by the hand of tyranny . . ." Following Bentham, Singer believes that all pleasures and pains, even of nonhumans, must be tallied for a proper moral calculus. He developed his position in several writings, including a widely read 1973 essay in the *New York Review of Books*.

Animal Suffering

In *Animal Liberation: A New Ethics for Our Treatment of Animals*, Singer argued that humans must take into account the fact that animals are capable of suffering and enjoyment. It is just as arbitrary to disregard the suffering of animals as that of women or people with dark skin. To assume that humans are inevitably superior to other species is "speciesism"—an injustice parallel to racism and sexism. Animals, in other words, are worthy of moral consideration: "What we must do is bring nonhuman animals within our sphere of moral concern and cease to treat their lives as expendable for whatever trivial purposes we may have." Articulating the intuitive feelings of those inclined toward sentimental anthropomorphism, Singer's plea for equal consideration has since become the principle of the movement, and "speciesism" has become a key catch word.

Singer did not, however, claim that all lives were of equal worth or that all beings should be treated in identical ways. It would make no sense to give a dog the right to vote, since dogs cannot understand what it means to vote. But dogs can feel pleasure and pain. It is this characteristic, Singer argued, that brings them into our moral calculus: "The basic principle of equality does not require equal or identical *treatment;* it requires equal *consideration.*" Beyond this right to equal consideration, however, Singer's utilitarian framework discourages discussion of absolute individual rights; it examines only aggregates, and views individuals less as autonomous actors than as sites for pleasures and pains. His critique of speciesism recognizes "that there are morally relevant differences between species—such as differences in mental capacities—and that they entitle us to give more weight to the interests of members of species with superior mental capacities." He denies, however, "that species membership *in itself* is a reason for giving more weight to the interests of one being than to those of another." Each individual being must be judged for its own particular capacities for pleasure.

Singer's utilitarian approach allows animal experimentation if suffering is minimized and the research has a high probability of yielding aggregate benefits that outweigh the individual pain. Nor does Singer unequivocally reject all animal products. It is permissible to eat free-range eggs, for these hens can "live comfortably. They do not appear to mind the removal of their eggs." He allows for differences between species in their sense of pain; it is probably permissible to eat an oyster but not a shrimp, but because we cannot know with certainty if mollusks feel pain, those who wish to be certain should avoid them as well. For Singer, then, suffering is the problem; the use of animals for human ends, if considerate and painless, is not in itself to be condemned.

A Call to Action

Animal Liberation contains far more than philosophical discussion. Half the book documents, in gruesome detail, what happens to animals used in agriculture and research.

The book also provides practical advice: vegetarian foods and cookbooks, names of animal organizations, and further reading. In effect a 300 page how-to guide, *Animal Liberation* played a crucial role in helping to form the animal rights agenda. For those already active and concerned with animals, it provided philosophical arguments and justification for what they wanted to do. It gave the incipient movement an ideology and a vocabulary. Joyce Tischler, then a law student and later founder of the Animal Legal Defense Fund, says: "Singer's book influenced us all. It gave us a philosophy on which to hang our emotions, feelings, sentimentality—all the things we had thought were bad; it gave us an intellectual hat to put on our heads." Activism for animals was no longer just compassion; it had recourse to systematic philosophical arguments. For people like Tischler, who had been active in other social movements—for women's rights, for environmental protection—a coherent ideology was an important part of political action.

Singer also opened up a new vista for animal protectionists. He pushed beyond the welfarist concentration on pets and the environmentalist concern with wild animals to pursue institutional abuses he thought would be hardest to stop. Singer felt animal abuse was an inevitable part of big business and science. He adapted the political attack on instrumentalism, an attack honed by environmentalists, to practices they had not considered.

Avon Books published an inexpensive paperback edition of *Animal Liberation* in 1977, and almost all animal rightists own a copy. When describing their conversion to animal rights, rank-and-file activists inevitably talk about Singer's book. They mention his critique of speciesism, and they reiterate his descriptions of cruel practices in factory farming and research laboratories. These descriptions have been more influential than his philosophical arguments. While many pragmatists in the movement accept Singer's philosophy, most fundamentalists reject his utilitarian position allowing the use of animals if anticipated benefits exceed the costs of suffering. While fundamentalists use his book in recruiting members, they find it too moderate. Singer is not an "animal person," many say. He has no particular fascination, interest, or love for animals, and no companion animals. One activist, herself living with eight cats, complained, "He's very highly evolved intellectually, but there's no emotion, no feeling. . . . He's cerebral, not an animal lover. . . . You'd think he could at least take an animal or two from the pound." The growing crusade for animals soon outpaced Singer's position, as protestors developed an uncompromising stand against any use of animals for human ends. Tom Regan emerged as the philosopher articulating the rights perspective of these fundamentalists.

A Second Theory

The same year Singer published *Animal Liberation*, Tom Regan, professor of philosophy at North Carolina State University, published an essay entitled "The Moral Basis of Vegetarianism." Regan had been trained in analytic philosophy, and his M.A. and Ph.D. theses, on beauty and goodness respectively, dealt with the meanings of the words rather than what was actually beautiful or good. The Vietnam war changed his academic approach, leading him to study pacifism and to explore Mohandas Gandhi's writings on animals and vegetarianism. Like Singer, Regan wanted to bring the insights of moral philosophy to politics and policy questions.

Gandhi and vegetarianism shaped Regan's intellectual trajectory; the death of his dog during the same summer was an emotional jolt. He writes, "My head had begun to grasp a moral truth that required a change in my behavior. Reason demanded that I become vegetarian. But it was the death of our dog that awakened my heart. It was that sense of irrecoverable loss that added the power of feeling to the requirements of logic." In a published interview Regan put it more tritely: "Philosophy can lead the mind to water but only emotion can make it drink." Regan's intellectual and political activities have focused ever since on animals; he has written and edited a stream of articles and books, and founded the Culture and Animals Foundation.

The Inherent Worth of Animals

In a position more extreme than Singer's, Regan argued that animals have inherent worth as living creatures, and should never be used as resources. Regan came to this view gradually; in a 1982 essay he admitted animals could be used in some experimental research. However, only a year later, he published his central treatise, *The Case for Animal Rights*, developing a more absolutist position that broke from utilitarianism. This view reflected the emerging sentiments of an increasing number of animal activists, as the philosophies of fundamentalists and pragmatists in the animal rights crusade began to diverge.

Regan built his case by arguing for the similarities between humans and other mammals, developing in effect the theoretical basis for a strongly sentimental anthropomorphism. From common sense, from the way animals behave, and from their evolutionary proximity to humans, we have every reason—according to Regan—to conclude that normal mammals have many complex aspects of consciousness, including perception, memory, beliefs, desires, preferences, intentions, and a sense of the future. They have needs and desires and organize their lives with the intention of satisfying them. Animals, argues Regan, are "subjects of a life," which they can perceive as going well or badly. Thus, like humans, they "have a value of their own," independent of their utility for humans. Inherent worth does not come in degrees; a creature either has it or does not. Having inherent worth gives an animal the absolute right to live its life with respect and autonomy. Regan explicitly attacks the utilitarian perspective: "On the rights view, we cannot justify harming a single rat merely by aggregating 'the many human and humane benefits' that flow from doing it." For Regan, the rat has worth beyond the benefits it can provide to humans.

Just as Singer argued that some animals may lack the capacity to feel pain, so Regan admitted that some animals may lack many attributes of consciousness. But since we do not know how aware they are, we must treat them all as conscious beings:

> We simply do not know enough to justify dismissing, *out of hand*, the idea that a frog, say, may be the subject-of-a-life, replete with desires, goals, beliefs, intentions, and the like. When our ignorance is so great, and the possible moral price so large, it is not unreasonable to give these animals the benefit of the doubt, treating them *as if* they are subjects, due our respectful treatment, especially when doing so causes no harm to us.

It is this willingness to attribute human qualities to frogs—to believe they may be conscious subjects and worthy of respect—that distinguishes animal rightists from the general public. . . .

Inalienable Rights

Regan believes that an uncompromising moral position is a better way to protect animals than Singer's utilitarianism: "Those who accept the rights view, and who sign for animals, will not be satisfied with anything less than the total abolition of the harmful use of animals in science—in education, in toxicity testing, in basic research." This was an appealing ideology for a moral crusade. It articulated the beliefs that already motivated many activists, it justified their goals in philosophical terms, and it reassured them as they tried to abolish animal exploitation.

A densely reasoned, 400-page philosophical text, *The Case for Animal Rights* did not win the readership of Singer's *Animal Liberation*. Most activists and many casual participants have read Singer's book; few Regan's. Even Regan admits that his book, "is a work of serious, methodical scholarship, written in the language of philosophy, 'direct duties,' 'acquired rights,' 'utilitarianism,' the whole lexicon of academic philosophy. It can be rough going for someone unfamiliar with the field, but I make no apologies for its difficulty. Physics is hard. In my view, moral philosophy is harder." Many people within the movement confuse the arguments of the two philosophers, adopting Regan's ideas but attributing them to Singer. Regan says "I cannot begin to count the number of times I have sat through discussions or read essays in which my views regarding the rights of animals were attributed, not to me, but to Singer." But despite the confusion, it is Regan's rights argument—not Singer's utilitarianism—that has come to dominate the rhetoric of the animal rights agenda, often pushing it beyond reformism and pragmatism. . . .

A Movement Grows

Singer, Regan, and [Mary] Midgley [an important British philosopher] helped generate a lively debate among professional philosophers, yielding both a popular and a professional literature in the late 1970s and 1980s that disseminated animal rights ideas. The Society for the Study of Ethics and Animals, founded in 1979, began holding annual meetings and established a journal, *Ethics and Animals*, for philosophical debates on animals and their treatment. In 1984, *Between the Species* began publishing a mixture of essays, interviews, and fiction dealing with the relationships between humans and other species. Several mainstream philosophy journals have had special issues on animal rights, including *Etyka* in Poland, *Inquiry* (Norway), *The Monist* and *Philosophy* (United Kingdom), and *Ethics* (United States).

While most philosophers have entered the animal rights debate purely as academics, others are activists as well, and it is often hard to distinguish between their intellectual and political activism. Steve Sapontzis, who teaches at California State University at Hayward, is an example. A vegetarian since his teens, he read Singer's book and Regan's article on vegetarianism around 1977, and his "personal and professional lives came together." He began teaching special courses on the ethics of animal use and, by 1981, was publishing articles and making speeches on the topic. A book followed in 1987, and he became co-editor of *Between the Species*. But in 1981, he was also involved in political action. After helping Elliot Katz found Californians for Responsible Research in 1983, Sapontzis soon left because he disagreed with Katz's ambitions to create a national organization (it became In Defense of Animals). He also helped Brad Miller start the Humane Farming Association; served on the Animal Welfare and Research Committee at the Lawrence Berkeley Laboratory; sits on the boards of the San Francisco Vegetarian Society, PAW PAC [California's Political Action Committee for Animals] , and the International Network for Religion and Animals; and is president of the Hayward Friends of Animals—a group devoted to improving conditions at the local shelter. Sapontzis' professional philosophy and his political activism reinforce each other. . . .

Explicit ideologies are vital to protest movements, giving form to shapeless feelings and reassuring participants about their grounds for acting. Sheer anger or frustration do not by themselves bring protestors into the streets. People need to link their feelings to an explanation, a cause, perhaps to a villain. And they need some vision of alternatives. Ideologies provide the rationale for social action.

That a handful of moral philosophers could help spark a powerful social movement suggests that they appealed to moral sentiments already widely spread. In their lives and their writings, the animal rights philosophers combined the emotional compassion driving the humane tradition with the critique of instrumentalism developed by the environmental movement. They appeared at a time when environmental and biomedical ethics were emerging as professional fields, bent on influencing public policy and social practice. This was heady stuff for philosophers disaffected with the analytic tradition. Singer, Regan and others were exhilarated to find that their profession could say something to nonprofessionals about how to live, and they wanted their writings to spawn social action. Though their ideas have not in fact coalesced into a single widely accepted ideology, they provided philosophies that could be used in recruiting new members, educating those already in the movement, and persuading policymakers and the public to change their values and practices. Activists were ready to apply these ideas to a series of specific arenas where they felt animals were being abused.

Equality for Animals

PETER SINGER

In 1975 the Australian philosopher Peter Singer published Animal Liberation, *which argued that animals deserved equal moral consideration. In the following excerpt from a 1985 essay, Singer explains the philosophy behind animal liberation. Singer argues that when we think about whether animals deserve moral consideration, it should make no difference that animals are less intelligent than human beings, nor that they lack the capacity for language. After all, he points out, no one thinks it is morally acceptable to hurt mentally handicapped people. What really matters, Singer says, is whether a being can feel pleasure and pain. If it can, then it deserves to have its interests considered equally with those of others. Singer notes that granting animals equality of consideration does not mean that animals will be granted all the rights normal adult human beings have, but he does think that it will require radical changes in our current lifestyles. Singer is currently the Ira W. DeCamp Professor of Bioethics at Princeton University's Center for Human Values.*

O ver the last few years, the public has gradually become aware of the existence of a new cause: animal liberation. Most people first heard of the movement through newspaper articles, often of the "what on earth will they come up with next?" variety. Then there were marches and demonstrations against factory farming, animal experimentation or the Canadian seal slaughter; all brought to an audience of millions by the TV cameras. Finally there have been the illegal acts: slogans daubed on fur shops, laboratories broken into and animals rescued. What are the ideas behind the animal liberation movement, and where is it heading? In this essay I shall try to answer these questions.

Let us start with some history, so that we can get some perspective on the animal liberation movement. Concern for animal suffering can be found in Hindu thought, and the Buddhist idea of compassion is a universal one, extending to animals as well as humans; but nothing similar is to be found in our Western traditions. There are a few laws indicating some awareness of animal welfare in the Old Testament, but nothing at all in the New, nor in mainstream Christianity for its first eighteen hundred years.

[The apostle] Paul scornfully rejected the thought that God might care about the welfare of oxen, and the incident of the Gadarene swine, in which Jesus is described as sending devils into a herd of pigs and making them drown themselves in the sea, is explained by Augustine as intended to teach us that we have no duties toward animals. This interpretation was accepted by Thomas Aquinas, who stated that the only possible objection to cruelty to animals was that it might lead to cruelty to humans—according to Aquinas there was nothing wrong *in itself* with making animals suffer. This became the official view of the Roman Catholic Church to such good—or bad—effect that as late as the middle of the nineteenth century, Pope Pius IX refused permission for the founding of a Society for the Prevention of Cruelty to Animals in Rome, on the ground that to grant permission would imply that human beings have duties to the lower creatures.

Even in England, which has a reputation for being dotty about animals, the first efforts to obtain legal protection for members of other species were made only 180 years ago. They were greeted with derision. *The Times* was so lacking in appreciation of the idea that the suffering of animals ought to be prevented, that it attacked proposed legislation that would stop the "sport" of bull-baiting. Said that august newspaper: "Whatever meddles with the private personal disposition of man's time or property is tyranny." Animals, clearly, were just property.

Limited Protection

That was in 1800, and that bill was defeated. It took another twenty years to get the first anti-cruelty law onto the British statute-books. To give any consideration at all to the interest of animals was a significant step beyond the idea that the boundary of our species is also the boundary of morality. Yet the step was a restricted one, because it did not challenge our right to make whatever *use* we choose of other species. Only cruelty—causing pain when there was no reason for doing so, merely sheer sadism or callous indifference—was prohibited. The farmers who deprive their pigs of room to move do not offend against this concept of cruelty, for they are only doing what they think necessary to producing bacon. Similarly the scientists who poison a hundred rats in order to find the lethal dose of some new flavouring agent for toothpaste are not cruel—only concerned to follow the accepted procedures for testing for the safety of new products.

The nineteenth century anti-cruelty movement was built on the assumption that the interests of nonhuman animals deserve protection only when serious human interests are not at stake. Animals remained very clearly "lower creatures"; human beings were quite distinct from, and infinitely far above, all forms of animal life. Should our interests conflict with theirs, there could be no doubt about whose interests must be sacrificed: in all cases, it would be the interests of the animals that had to yield.

The significance of the new animal liberation movement is its challenge to this assumption. Animal liberationists have dared to question the right of our species to assume that human interests must always prevail. They have sought—absurd as it must sound at first—to extend such notions as equality and rights to nonhuman animals.

The Case for Animal Equality

How plausible is this extension? Is it really possible to take seriously the slogan of [George] Orwell's *Animal Farm:* "All Animals Are Equal"? The animal liberationists contend that it is; but in order to avoid hopelessly misunderstanding what they mean by this, we need to digress for a moment, to discuss the general ideal of equality.

It will be helpful to begin with the more familiar claim that all human beings are equal. When we say that all human beings, whatever their race, creed or sex are equal, what is it that we are asserting? Those who wish to defend a hierarchical, inegalitarian society have often pointed out that by whatever test we choose, it simply is not true that all humans are equal. Like it or not, we must face the fact that humans come in different shapes and sizes; they come with differing moral capacities, differing intellectual abilities, differing amounts of benevolent feeling and sensitivity to the needs of others, differing abilities to communicate effectively, and different capacities to experience pleasure and pain. In short, if the demand for equality were based on the actual equality of all human beings, we would have to stop demanding equality. It would be an unjustifiable demand.

Fortunately the case for upholding the equality of human beings does not depend on equality of intelligence, moral capacity, physical strength, or any other matters of fact of this kind. Equality is a moral ideal, not a simple assertion of fact. There is no logically compelling reason for assuming that a factual difference in ability between two people justifies any difference in the amount of consideration we give to satisfying their needs and interests. The principle of equality of human beings is not a description of an alleged actual equality: it is a prescription of how we should treat human beings.

[The philosopher] Jeremy Bentham incorporated the essential basis or moral equality into his utilitarian system of ethics in the formula: "Each to count for one and none for more than one". In other words, the interests of every being affected by an action are to be taken into account and given the same weight as the like interests of any other being.

It is an implication of this principle of equality that our concern for others ought not to depend on what they are like, or what abilities they possess—although precisely what this concern requires us to do may vary according to the characteristics of those affected by what we do. It is on this basis that the case against racism and the case against sexism must both ultimately rest; and it is in accordance with this principle that speciesism is also to be condemned. If possessing a higher degree of intelligence does not entitle one human being to use another for its own ends, how can it entitle human beings to exploit nonhuman beings?

Many philosophers have proposed the principle of equal consideration of interests in some form or other, as a basic moral principle; but not many of them have recognised that this principle applies to members of other species as well as to our own. Bentham was one of the few who did realise this. In a forward-looking passage, written at a time when black slaves in the British dominions were still being treated much as we now treat nonhuman animals, Bentham wrote:

> the day may come when the rest of the animal creation may acquire those rights which never could have been withholden from them but by the hand of tyranny. The French have already discovered that the blackness of the skin is no reason why a human being should be abandoned without redress to the caprice of a tormentor. It may one day come to be recognised that the number of the legs, the villosity of the skin, or the termination of the os sacrum, are reasons equally insufficient for abandoning a sensitive being to the same fate. What else is it that should trace the insuperable line? It is the faculty of reason, or perhaps the faculty of discourse? But a full-grown horse or dog is beyond comparison a more rational, as well as a more conversable animal, than an infant of a day, or a week, or even a month, old. But sup-

pose they were otherwise, what would it avail? the question is not, Can they reason? nor Can they talk but, Can they suffer?

In this passage Bentham points to the capacity for suffering as the vital characteristic that gives a being the right to equal consideration. The capacity for suffering—or more strictly, for suffering and/or enjoyment of happiness—is not just another characteristic like the capacity for language, or for higher mathematics. Bentham is not saying that those who try to mark "the insuperable line" that determines whether the interests of a being should be considered happen to have selected the wrong characteristic. The capacity for suffering and enjoying things is a pre-requisite for having interests at all, a condition that must be satisfied before we can speak of interests in any meaningful way. It would be nonsense to say that it was not in the interests of a stone to be kicked along the road by a child. A stone does not have interests because it cannot suffer. Nothing that we can do to it could possibly make any difference to its welfare. A mouse, on the other hand, does have an interest in not being tormented, because it will suffer if it is.

If a being suffers, there can be no moral justification for refusing to take that suffering into consideration. No matter what the nature of the being, the principle of equality requires that its suffering be counted equally with the like suffering—in so far as rough comparisons can be made—of any other being. If a being is not capable of suffering, or of experiencing enjoyment or happiness, there is nothing to be taken into account. This is why the limit of sentience (using the term as a convenient, if not strictly accurate, shorthand for the capacity to suffer or experience enjoyment or happiness) is the only defensible boundary of concern for the interests of others. To mark this boundary by some characteristic like intelligence or rationality would be to mark it in an arbitrary way. Why not choose some other characteristic, like skin colour?

Racists violate the principle of equality by giving greater

weight to the interests of members of their own race, when there is a clash between their interests and the interests of those of another race. Similarly speciesists allow the interests of their own species to override the greater interests of members of other species.

Equal Consideration of Interests

If the case for animal equality is sound, what follows from it? It does not follow, of course, that animals ought to have all of the rights that we think humans ought to have—including, for instance, the right to vote. It is equality of consideration of interests, not equality of rights, that the case for animal equality seeks to establish. But what exactly does this mean, in practical terms? It needs to be spelled out a little.

If I give a horse a hard slap across its rump with my open hand, the horse may start, but presumably feels little pain. Its skin is thick enough to protect it against a mere slap. If I slap a baby in the same way, however, the baby will cry and presumably does feel pain, for its skin is more sensitive. So it is worse to slap a baby than a horse, if both slaps are administered with equal force. But there must be some kind of blow—I don't know exactly what it would be, but perhaps a blow with a heavy stick—that would cause the horse as much pain as we cause a baby by slapping it with our hand. That is what I mean by the same amount of pain; and if we consider it wrong to inflict that much pain on a baby for no good reason then we must, unless we are speciesists, consider it equally wrong to inflict the same amount of pain on a horse for no good reason.

There are other differences between humans and animals that cause other complications. Normal adult human beings have mental capacities which will, in certain circumstances, lead them to suffer more than animals would in the same circumstances. If, for instance, we decided to perform extremely painful or lethal scientific experiments on normal adult humans, kidnapped at random from public parks for this purpose, every adult who entered a park would become fearful that he or she would be kidnapped. The resultant terror would be a form of suffering additional to the pain of the experiment.

The same experiments performed on nonhuman animals would cause less suffering since the animals would not have the anticipatory dread of being kidnapped and experimented upon. This does not mean, of course, that it would be *right* to perform the experiment on animals, but only that there is a reason, which is *not* speciesist, for preferring to use animals rather than normal adult humans, if the experiment is to be done at all. It should be noted, however, that this same argument gives us a reason for preferring to use human infants—orphans perhaps—or retarded human beings for experiments, rather than adults, since infants and retarded human beings would also have no idea of what was going to happen to them.

So far as this argument is concerned nonhuman animals and infants and retarded human beings are in the same category; and if we use this argument to justify experiments on nonhuman animals we have to ask ourselves whether we are also prepared to allow experiments on human infants and retarded adults; and if we make a distinction between animals and these humans, on what basis can we do it, other than a bare-faced—and morally indefensible—preference for members of our own species?

There are many areas in which the superior mental powers of normal adult human beings make a difference: anticipation, more detailed memory, greater knowledge of what is happening, and so on. Yet these differences do not all point to greater suffering on the part of the normal human being. Sometimes animals may suffer more because of their more limited understanding. If, for instance, we are taking prisoners in wartime we can explain to them that while they must submit to capture, search and confinement they will not otherwise be harmed and will be set free at the conclusion of hostilities. If we capture a wild animal, however, we cannot explain that we are not threatening its life. A wild animal cannot distinguish an attempt to over-power and confine from an attempt to kill; the one causes as much terror as the other.

It may be objected that comparisons of sufferings of different species are impossible to make, and that for this reason when the interests of animals and human beings clash the principle of equality gives no guidance. It is probably true that comparisons of suffering between members of different species cannot be made precisely, but precision is not essential. Even if we were to prevent the infliction of suffering on animals only when it is quite certain that the interests of human beings will not be affected, we would be forced to make radical changes in our treatment of animals that would involve our diet, the farming methods we use, experimental procedures in many fields of science, our approach to wildlife and to hunting, trapping and the wearing of furs, and areas of entertainment like circuses, rodeos, and zoos. As a result a vast amount of suffering would be avoided.

Killing Versus Harming

So far I have said a lot about the infliction of suffering on animals, but nothing about killing them. This omission has been deliberate. The application of the principle of equality to the infliction of suffering is, in theory at least, fairly straightforward. Pain and suffering are bad and should he prevented or minimised, irrespective of the race, sex, or species of the being that suffers. How bad a pain is depends on how intense it is and how long it lasts, but pains of the same magnitude are equally bad regardless of species.

While self-awareness, intelligence, the capacity for meaningful relations with others, and so on are not relevant to the question of inflicting pain—since pain is pain, whatever other capacities, beyond the capacity to feel pain, the being may have—these capacities may be relevant to the question of taking life. It is not arbitrary to hold that the life of a self-aware being, capable of abstract thought, of planning for the future, of complex acts of communication, and so on, is more valuable than the life of a being without these capacities.

To see the difference between the issues of inflicting pain and taking life, consider how we would choose within our own species. If we had to choose to save the life of the normal human being or a mentally defective human being, we would probably choose to save the life of the normal one; but if we had to choose between preventing pain in the normal human being or in the mentally defective— imagine that both have received painful but superficial injuries, and we only have enough painkiller for one of them—it is not nearly so clear how we ought to choose. The same is true when we consider other species. The evil of pain is, in itself, unaffected by the other characteristics of the being that feels the pain; the value of life is affected by these other characteristics.

Normally this will mean that if we have to choose between the life of a human being and the life of another animal we should choose to save the life of the human being; but there may be special cases in which the reverse holds true, because the human being in question does not have the capacities of a normal human being. So this view is not speciesist, although it may appear to be at first glance.

The preference, in normal cases, for saving a human life over the life of an animal when a choice *has* to be made is a preference based on the characteristics that normal human beings have and not on the mere fact that they are members of our own species. This is why when we consider members of our own species who lack the characteristics of normal human beings we can no longer say that their lives are always to be preferred to those of other animals. In general, though, the question of when it is wrong to kill (painlessly) an animal is one to which we need give no precise answer. As long as we remember that we should give the same respect to the lives of animals as we give to the lives of those human beings at a similar mental level we shall not go far wrong.

Humans Should Be Biased Toward Humans

WILLIAM TIMBERLAKE

In the following article, William Timberlake argues that Peter Singer's influential arguments supporting animal rights rest on a mistake. Timberlake notes that Singer says that most people traditionally accept that all humans are morally equal, in the sense that they deserve to be treated equally, and that all humans are morally superior to animals, in the sense that all humans deserve to have their interests considered above those of animals. Timberlake argues that Singer is wrong to assume most people believe this, as he says it is common to make distinctions, even among human beings, as to moral status. Furthermore, and more importantly, Timberlake challenges Singer's contention that there is no morally relevant property that all humans possess and that all animals lack. According to Timberlake, the property in question is human DNA. According to Timberlake, humans are justified in giving preferential treatment toward other human beings because if they did not, they would endanger the future of the human gene pool. Timberlake is a professor of psychology at Indiana University.

Singer, like other animal rights advocates, is not concerned with the definition of suffering. Rather, his concern is that animal suffering exists and that we should treat

William Timberlake, "The Attribution of Suffering," *Behavioral and Brain Sciences*, vol. 13, March 1980, pp. 36–39. Copyright © 1980 by Cambridge University Press. Reproduced by permission of Cambridge University Press and the author.

it the same as our own suffering. At first glance, failing to distinguish between the suffering of humans and the suffering of ticks, tapeworms, and maggots does not seem like a plausible position. There are hints that Singer intends ultimately to measure the intensity of suffering to make difficult decisions about relative suffering. But this is not included in the form of his main arguments, and it is certainly not the way his arguments have been used by animal rights advocates.

Singer begins with the assumption that animal suffering is rampant because of our Judeo-Christian heritage, which gives humans "dominion" over animals. According to Singer, in this tradition "human beings have a divine warrant for always giving priority to human interests." I am neither a biblical scholar nor a historian, but as I remember it, the meaning of dominion here implies responsibility as well as authority. Certainly farmers who espouse the Judeo-Christian ethic have risked their lives for their animals, and provided them at times with equal or even privileged access to scarce resources of food and shelter. I believe that the concern of many ecologists about disappearing species comes partly from a sense of the responsibility of human dominion over the planet. The animal rights movement itself appears to have roots in the Judeo-Christian beliefs of the unique responsibility of humans for animals and the obligation to deny impulses to gain advantage over those who are less powerful than ourselves.

Singer attacks the Judeo-Christian ethic for producing two highly influential but contradictory moral principles: (1) All humans are equal in moral status; (2) all humans are superior in moral status to nonhuman animals. According to Singer, these assumptions are incompatible because their joint truth requires the existence of some common quality that is possessed by humans, making them equal, and is not possessed by animals. Singer then argues that because there is no such quality, we must give the same effort to the elimination of suffering in animals as we do to the elimination of suffering in humans.

Moral Inequality

There are many problems with this approach. First, I'm not clear these are common assumptions. I do not believe that people commonly assume that all humans are equal in moral status or even that all humans are better than all animals. Equality of moral status is something we aspire to in specific circumstances; we have tried to formalize those circumstances in legal systems, but a few moments of conversation with the average person should convince one that this is not a common belief. Children do not have the moral status of adults, the mentally ill are not judged by the same standards as the mentally competent, illegal immigrants do not have the moral status of citizens, nonresident poor do not have the moral status of resident poor, strangers do not have the moral status of friends, someone who has stolen from us does not have the moral status of someone who has befriended us. A fairer summary of what we commonly believe is that only within certain boundaries and in certain dimensions are humans assumed to be similar in moral status, and usually only in the absence of further information.

I believe we commonly place nonhuman animals in the same framework. For example, both people and animals that are judged nobler or more intelligent are often accorded higher moral status. In a not inconsequential number of cases, some animals may be viewed as nobler than some or even most humans. When we add to this an overall bias toward viewing beings that are more similar to or related to ourselves as nobler or more intelligent than beings that are distantly removed from us, we have a complex set of assumptions influencing the judgments of differences in the moral status of both human and nonhuman animals. There is no necessary discontinuity between our moral evaluations of animals and humans and, thus, no logical problem. Both human and nonhuman animals may be ranked differently and with overlap in moral status depending on the dimensions and circumstances.

The Importance of DNA

The second problem with Singer's approach is that there *is* a common quality that unites humans and separates them from animals, namely, the unique aspects of DNA found in human cells. Singer might well argue here that we cannot specify perfectly the nature of the human gene pool, and that even if we could, it would simply be a species identification and not a logical reason for making judgments of the relative value of suffering. As far as I can see, however, the existence of even modestly distinct pools of DNA must be based on pressures toward reproduction within that restricted set of genes. At least some of this pressure will take the form of choices that effectively value the suffering and survival of gene pool representatives more than the suffering, survival, and reproduction of some other set of animals having an alternative gene pool. If this is not so, either the amount of resources in the world is infinite, or the particular gene pool in question will not long be with us.

I am not arguing that all acts necessarily have immediate or even long-term benefits to a particular gene pool. Social species, perhaps especially humans, make choices that benefit the survival and reproduction of genetically dissimilar animals. But the variables controlling these acts of altruism more often than not do produce results of long-term benefit to the human gene pool. Thus, though all acts of individual animals may not contribute to the reproduction of their own genes, if we consider all acts controlled by similar variables across all individuals from a gene pool, that is the expected direction.

Singer might well acknowledge that this is the status of the world, yet argue that it should be different. The moral status and suffering of an animal should count the same as those of humans to every human evaluator. Appealing though it may be, this view is neither logically consistent nor viable. Consider the incompatibility of the following beliefs: (1) All animals (including humans) are equal in moral status; (2) all animals except humans can promote the survival of their own kind at the expense of the suffering and restricted access to resources of other species. First, it follows from statement (1) that humans have the same rights as predators to express their predatory tendencies. But it follows from statement (2) that they must not express these tendencies. Therefore, the moral status of humans is either higher or lower than that of other animals, but definitely different.

A second argument is similar. On the grounds of evolution, the rule that all animals are equal in moral status is literally not viable. Every animal on the planet is competing for resources with other animals. Even the most devout human vegetarian living alone with minimal shelter, few clothes, and great respect for life is denying resources critical to the survival and reproduction of a surprisingly large number of animals by his simple presence in the ecosystem. If he has a dog or a cat as a pet, so much the worse for other animals.

In short, the logic of our Judeo-Christian heritage is certainly no more flawed than that of the animal rights approach (which in part represents an extension of pieces of that heritage). Both animal rights advocates and scientists want to reduce the suffering of others, but this cannot be done in any reasonable way until we agree on its nature, extent, and relative value.

Animals Have Inherent Value

TOM REGAN

In the following piece, philosopher Tom Regan argues that animals are like humans in being what he calls subjects of a life. *Regan begins by noting that traditional views state that people are obliged to consider animals as property. According to this model, Regan says, the reason it is wrong to harm an animal is similar to the reason it is wrong to destroy someone's car. In both cases, on this traditional model, the act is wrong because it harms the person who owns the thing that is harmed, be it an animal or a car. Regan rejects this view and argues that we have a duty not to harm animals because doing so violates their rights by failing to recognize their inherent value. Regan distinguishes his view from the utilitarianism advocated by Peter Singer, another prominent supporter of animal rights. Utilitarianism is the view that one has to produce the best outcome for everyone involved, and Singer argues that the interests of animals deserve equal consideration in the calculation. That is, according to this utilitarian view, if the morally good action is the one that produces the best outcome, the best outcome is the one that is best for human beings and animals considered on an equal footing. Regan objects to this view by noting that the view makes it morally acceptable to do great harm to someone if doing so produces enough good for other people. Regan rejects this, and argues that both human beings and animals have rights that cannot be violated, even if violating them would produce*

---

a lot of good for other people or animals. Regan is professor of philosophy at North Carolina State University.

I regard myself as an advocate of animal rights—as a part of the animal rights movement. That movement, as I conceive it, is committed to a number of goals, including:
- the total abolition of the use of animals in science;
- the total dissolution of commercial animal agriculture;
- the total elimination of commercial and sport hunting and trapping.

There are, I know, people who profess to believe in animal rights but do not avow these goals. Factory farming, they say, is wrong—it violates animals' rights—but traditional animal agriculture is all right. Toxicity tests of cosmetics on animals violates their rights, but important medical research—cancer research, for example—does not. The clubbing of baby seals is abhorrent, but not the harvesting of adult seals. I used to think I understood this reasoning. Not any more. You don't change unjust institutions by tidying them up.

What's wrong—fundamentally wrong—with the way animals are treated isn't the details that vary from case to case. It's the whole system. The forlornness of the veal calf is pathetic, heart wrenching; the pulsing pain of the chimp with electrodes planted deep in her brain is repulsive; the slow, torturous death of a raccoon caught in the leg-hold trap is agonizing. But what is wrong isn't the pain, isn't the suffering, isn't the deprivation. These compound what's wrong. Sometimes—often—they make it much worse. But they are not the fundamental wrong.

The Fundamental Wrong

The fundamental wrong is the system that allows us to view animals as *our resources*, here for *us*—to be eaten, or surgically manipulated, or exploited for sport or money. Once we accept this view of animals—as our resources—the rest is as predictable as it is regrettable. Why worry about their loneliness, their pain, their death? Since animals exist for us, to benefit us in one way or another, what harms them really doesn't matter—or matters only if it starts to bother us, makes us feel a trifle uneasy when we eat our veal escalope, for example. So, yes, let us get veal calves out of solitary confinement, give them more space, a little straw, a few companions. But let us keep our veal escalope.

But a little straw, more space and a few companions won't eliminate—won't even touch—the basic wrong that attaches to our viewing and treating these animals as our resources. A veal calf killed to be eaten after living in close confinement is viewed and treated in this way: but so, too, is another who is raised (as they say) "more humanely". To right the wrong of our treatment of farm animals requires more than making rearing methods "more humane"; it requires the total dissolution of commercial animal agriculture. . . .

The Traditional View

How to proceed? We begin by asking how the moral status of animals has been understood by thinkers who deny that animals have rights. Then we test the mettle of their ideas by seeing how well they stand up under the heat of fair criticism. If we start our thinking in this way, we soon find that some people believe that we have no direct duties to animals, that we owe nothing to them, that we can do nothing that wrongs them. Rather, we can do wrong acts that involve animals, and so we have duties regarding them, though none to them. Such views may be called indirect duty views. By way of illustration: suppose your neighbor kicks your dog. Then your neighbor has done something wrong. But not to your dog. The wrong that has been done is a wrong to you. After all, it is wrong to upset people, and your neighbor's kicking your dog upsets you. So you are the one who is wronged, not your dog. Or again: by kicking your dog your neighbor damages your property. And since it is wrong to damage another person's property, your neighbor has done something wrong—to you, of course—not to your dog. Your neighbor no more wrongs your dog than your car would be wronged if the windshield were smashed. Your neighbor's duties involving your dog are indirect duties to you. More generally, all of our duties regarding animals are indirect duties to one another—to humanity.

How could someone try to justify such a view? Someone might say that your dog doesn't feel anything and so isn't hurt by your neighbor's kick, doesn't care about the pain because none is felt, is as unaware of anything as is your windshield. Someone might say this, but no rational person will, since, among other considerations, such a view will commit anyone who holds it to the position that no human being feels pain either—that human beings also don't care about what happens to them. A second possibility is that though both humans and your dog are hurt when kicked, it is only human pain that matters. But, again, no rational person can believe this. Pain is pain wherever it occurs. If your neighbor's causing you pain is wrong because of the pain that is caused, we cannot rationally ignore or dismiss the moral relevance of the pain that your dog feels.

Philosophers who hold indirect duty views—and many still do—have come to understand that they must avoid the two defects just noted: that is, both the view that animals don't feel anything as well as the idea that only human pain can be morally relevant. Among such thinkers the sort of view now favoured is one or other form of what is called *contractarianism*.

Morality as a Contract

Here, very crudely, is the root idea: morality consists of a set of rules that individuals voluntarily agree to abide by, as we do when we sign a contract (hence the name contractarianism). Those who understand and accept the terms of the contract are covered directly; they have rights created and recognized by, and protected in, the contract. And these contractors can also have protection spelled out for others who, though they lack the ability to understand morality and so cannot sign the contract themselves, are loved or cherished by those who can. Thus young children, for example, are unable to sign contracts and lack rights. But they are protected by the contract nonetheless because of the sentimental interests of others, most notably their parents. So we have, then, duties involving these children, duties regarding them, but no duties to them. Our duties in this case are indirect duties to other human beings, usually their parents.

As for animals, since they cannot understand contracts, they obviously cannot sign; and since they cannot sign, they have no rights. Like children, however, some animals are the objects of the sentimental interest of others. You, for example, love your dog or cat. So those animals that enough people care about (companion animals, whales, baby seals, the American bald eagle), though they lack rights themselves, will be protected because of the sentimental interests of people. I have, then, according to contractarianism, no duty directly to your dog or any other animal, not even the duty not to cause them pain or suffering; my duty not to hurt them is a duty I have to those people who care about what happens to them. As for other animals, where no or little sentimental interest is present—in the case of farm animals, for example, or laboratory rats—what duties we have grow weaker and weaker, perhaps to the vanishing point. The pain and death they endure, though real, are not wrong if no one cares about them.

A Problem with the View

When it comes to the moral status of animals, contractarianism could be a hard view to refute if it were an adequate theoretical approach to the moral status of human beings. It is not adequate in this latter respect, however, which makes the question of its adequacy in the former case, regarding animals, utterly moot. For consider: morality, according to the (crude) contractarian position before us, consists of rules that people agree to abide by. What people? Well, enough to make a difference—enough, that is, *collectively* to have the power to enforce the rules that are drawn up in the contract. That is very well and good for the signatories but not so good for anyone who is not asked to sign. And there is nothing in contractarianism of the sort we are discussing that guarantees or requires that everyone will have a chance to participate equally in framing the rules of morality. The result is that this approach to ethics could sanction the most blatant forms of social, economic, moral and political injustice, ranging from a repressive caste system to systematic racial or sexual discrimination. Might, according to this theory, does make right. Let those who are the victims of injustice suffer as they will. It matters not so long as no one else—no contractor, or too few of them—cares about it. Such a theory takes one's moral breath away . . . as if, for example, there would be nothing wrong with apartheid in South Africa if few white South Africans were upset by it. A theory with so little to recommend it at the level of the ethics of our treatment of our fellow humans cannot have anything more to recommend it when it comes to the ethics of how we treat our fellow animals. . . .

Indirect duty views, then, including the best among them, fail to command our rational assent. Whatever ethical theory we should accept rationally, therefore, it must at least recognize that we have some duties directly to animals, just as we have some duties directly to each other. The next two theories I'll sketch attempt to meet this requirement.

Cruelty and Kindness

The first I call the cruelty-kindness view. Simply stated, this says that we have a direct duty to be kind to animals and a direct duty not to be cruel to them. Despite the familiar, reassuring ring of these ideas, I do not believe that this view offers an adequate theory. To make this clearer, consider kindness. A kind person acts from a certain kind of motive—compassion or concern, for example. And that is a virtue. But there is no guarantee that a kind act is a right act. If I am a generous racist, for example, I will be inclined to act kindly towards members of my own race, favouring their interests above those of others. My kindness would be real and, so far as it goes, good. But I trust it is too obvious to require argument that my kind acts may not be above moral reproach—may, in fact, be positively wrong because rooted in injustice. So kindness, notwithstanding its status as a virtue to be encouraged, simply will not carry the weight of a theory of right action.

Cruelty fares no better. People or their acts are cruel if they display either a lack of sympathy or, worse, the presence of enjoyment in another's suffering. Cruelty in all its guises is a bad thing, a tragic human failing. But just as a person's being motivated by kindness does not guarantee that he or she does what is right, so the absence of cruelty does not ensure that he or she avoids doing what is wrong. Many people who perform abortions, for example, are not cruel, sadistic people. But that fact alone does not settle the terribly difficult question of the morality of abortion. The case is no different when we examine the ethics of our treatment of animals. So, yes, let us be for kindness and against cruelty. But let us not suppose that being for the one and against the other answers questions about moral right and wrong.

The Trouble with Utilitarianism

Some people think that the theory we are looking for is utilitarianism. A utilitarian accepts two moral principles. The first is that of equality: everyone's interests count, and similar interests must be counted as having similar weight or importance. White or black, American or Iranian, human or animal—everyone's pain or frustration matter, and matter just as much as the equivalent pain or frustration of anyone else. The second principle a utilitarian accepts is that of utility: do the act that will bring about the best balance between satisfaction and frustration for everyone affected by the outcome.

As a utilitarian, then, here is how I am to approach the task of deciding what I morally ought to do: I must ask who will be affected if I choose to do one thing rather than another, how much each individual will be affected, and where the best results are most likely to lie—which option, in other words, is most likely to bring about the best results, the best balance between satisfaction and frustration. That option, whatever it may be, is the one I ought to choose. That is where my moral duty lies.

The great appeal of utilitarianism rests with its uncompromising *egalitarianism:* everyone's interests count and count as much as the like interests of everyone else. The kind of odious discrimination that some forms of contractarianism can justify—discrimination based on race or sex, for example—seems disallowed in principle by utilitarianism, as is speciesism, systematic discrimination based on species membership. . . .

Serious problems arise for utilitarianism when we remind ourselves that it enjoins us to bring about the best consequences. What does this mean? It doesn't mean the best consequences for me alone, or for my family or friends, or any other person taken individually. No, what we must do is, roughly, as follows: we must add up (somehow!) the separate satisfactions and frustrations of everyone likely to be affected by our choice, the satisfactions in one column, the frustrations in the other. We must total each column for each of the options before us. That is what it means to say the theory is aggregative. And then we must choose that option which is most likely to bring about the best balance of totaled satisfactions over totaled frustrations. Whatever act would lead to this outcome is the one we ought morally to perform—it is where our moral duty lies. And that act quite clearly might not be the same one that would bring about the best results for me personally, or for my family or friends, or for a lab animal. The best aggregated consequences for everyone concerned are not necessarily the best for each individual.

That utilitarianism is an aggregative theory—different individuals' satisfactions or frustrations are added, or summed, or totaled—is the key objection to this theory. My Aunt Bea is old, inactive, a cranky, sour person, though not physically ill. She prefers to go on living. She is also rather rich. I could make a fortune if I could get my hands on her money, money she intends to give me in any event, after she dies, but which she refuses to give me now. In order to avoid a huge tax bite, I plan to donate a handsome sum of my profits to the local children's hospital. Many, many children will benefit from my generosity, and much joy will be brought to their parents, relatives and friends. If I don't get the money rather soon, all these ambitions will come to naught. The once-in-a-lifetime opportunity to make a real killing will be gone. Why, then, not kill my Aunt Bea? Of course, I *might* get caught. But I'm no fool and, besides, her doctor can be counted on to cooperate (he has an eye for the same investment and I happen to know a good deal about his shady past). The deed can be done . . . professionally, shall we say. There is *very* little chance of getting caught. And as for my conscience being guilt-ridden, I am a resourceful sort of fellow and will take more than sufficient comfort—as I lie on the beach at Acapulco—in contemplating the joy and health I have brought to so many others.

Suppose Aunt Bea is killed and the rest of the story comes out as told. Would I have done anything wrong? Anything immoral? One would have thought that I had. Not according to utilitarianism. Since what I have done has brought about the best balance between totaled satisfaction and frustration for all those affected by the outcome, my action is not wrong. Indeed, in killing Aunt Bea the physician and I did what duty required.

This same kind of argument can be repeated in all sorts of cases, illustrating, time after time, how the utilitarian's position leads to results that impartial people find morally callous. It *is* wrong to kill my Aunt Bea in the name of bringing about the best results for others. A good end does not justify an evil means. Any adequate moral theory will have to explain why this is so. Utilitarianism fails in this respect and so cannot be the theory we seek.

A Better Theory of Rights

What to do? Where to begin anew? The place to begin, I think, is with the utilitarian's view of the value of the individual—or, rather, lack of value. In its place, suppose we consider that you and I, for example, do have value as individuals—what we'll call *inherent value.* To say we have such value is to say that we are something more than, something different from, mere receptacles. Moreover, to ensure that we do not pave the way for such injustices as slavery or sexual discrimination, we must believe that all who have inherent value have it equally, regardless of their sex, race, religion, birthplace and so on. Similarly to be discarded as irrelevant are one's talents or skills, intelligence and wealth, personality or pathology, whether one is loved and admired or despised and loathed. The genius and the retarded child, the prince and the pauper, the brain surgeon and the fruit vendor, Mother Teresa and the most unscrupulous used-car salesman—all have inherent value, all possess it equally, and all have an equal right to be treated with respect, to be treated in ways that do not reduce them to the status of things, as if they existed as resources for others. My value as an individual is independent of my usefulness to you. Yours is not dependent on your usefulness to me. For either of us to treat the other in ways that fail to show respect for the other's independent value is to act immorally, to violate the individual's rights.

Some of the rational virtues of this view—what I call the rights view—should be evident. Unlike (crude) contractarianism, for example, the rights view *in principle* denies the moral tolerability of any and all forms of racial, sexual or social discrimination; and unlike utilitarianism, this view *in principle* denies that we can justify good results by using evil means that violate an individual's rights—denies, for example, that it could be moral to kill my Aunt Bea to harvest beneficial consequences for others. That would be to sanction the disrespectful treatment of the individual in the name of the social good, something the rights view will not—categorically will not—ever allow.

The rights view, I believe, is rationally the most satisfactory moral theory. It surpasses all other theories in the degree to which it illuminates and explains the foundations of our duties to one another—the domain of human morality. On this score it has the best reasons, the best arguments, on its side. Of course, if it were possible to show that only human beings are included within its scope, then a person like myself, who believes in animal rights, would be obliged to look elsewhere.

What Humans and Animals Share

But attempts to limit its scope to humans only can be shown to be rationally defective. Animals, it is true, lack many of the abilities humans possess. They can't read, do higher mathematics, build a bookcase or make *baba ghanoush.* Neither can many human beings, however, and yet we don't (and shouldn't) say that they (these humans) therefore have less inherent value, less of a right to be treated with respect, than do others. It is the *similarities* between those human beings who most clearly, most non-controversially have such value (the people reading this, for example), not our differences, that matter most. And the real crucial, the basic similarity is simply this: we are each of us the experiencing subject of a life, a conscious creature having an individual welfare that has importance to us whatever our usefulness to others. We want and prefer things, believe and feel things, recall and expect things. And all these dimensions of our life, including our pleasure and pain, our enjoyment and suffering, our satisfaction and frustration, our continued existence or our untimely death—all make a difference to the quality of our life as lived, as experienced, by us as individuals. As the same is true of those animals that concern us (the ones that are eaten and trapped, for example), they too must be viewed as the experiencing subjects of a life, with inherent value of their own.

Some there are who resist the idea that animals have inherent value. "Only humans have such value", they profess. How might this narrow view be defended? Shall we say that only humans have the requisite intelligence, or autonomy, or reason? But there are many, many humans who fail to meet these standards and yet are reasonably viewed as having value above and beyond their usefulness to others. Shall we claim that only humans belong to the right species, the species *Homo sapiens*? But this is blatant speciesism. Will it be said, then, that all—and only—humans have immortal souls? Then our opponents have their work cut out for them. I am myself not ill-disposed to the proposition that there are immortal souls. Personally, I profoundly hope I have one. But I would not want to rest my position on a controversial ethical issue or the even more controversial question about who or what has an immortal soul. That is to dig one's hole deeper, not to climb out. Rationally, it is better to resolve moral issues without making more controversial assumptions than are needed. The question of who has inherent value is such a question, one that is resolved more rationally without the introduction of the idea of immortal souls than by its use.

The Equality of Inherent Value

Well, perhaps some will say that animals have some inherent value, only less than we have. Once again, however, attempts to defend this view can be shown to lack rational justification. What could be the basis of our having more inherent value than animals? Their lack of reason, or autonomy, or intellect? Only if we are willing to make the same judgement in the case of humans who are similarly deficient. But it is not true that such humans—the retarded child, for example, or the mentally deranged—have less inherent value than you or I. Neither, then, can we rationally sustain the view that animals like them in being the experiencing subjects of a life have less inherent value. *All* who have inherent value have it *equally*, whether they be human animals or not.

Inherent value, then, belongs equally to those who are the experiencing subjects of a life. Whether it belongs to others—to rocks and rivers, trees and glaciers, for example—we do not know and may never know. But neither do we need to know, if we are to make the case for animal rights. We do not need to know, for example, how many people are eligible to vote in the next presidential election before we can know whether I am. Similarly, we do not need to know how many individuals have inherent value before we can know that some do. When it comes to the case for animal rights, then, what we need to know is whether the animals that, in our culture, are routinely eaten, hunted and used in our laboratories, for example, are like us in being subjects of a life. And we do know this. We do know that many—literally, billions and billions—of these animals are the subjects of a life in the sense explained and so have inherent value if we do. And since, in order to arrive at the best theory of our duties to one another, we must recognize our equal inherent value as individuals, reason—not sentiment, not emotion—reason compels us to recognize the equal inherent value of these animals and, with this, their equal right to be treated with respect.

Animal Rights Are Weaker than Human Rights

MARY ANNE WARREN

In the following piece, Mary Anne Warren argues that there is good reason to believe human beings have more rights than animals do. Warren develops her position by arguing that the theory developed by the philosopher Tom Regan, which Warren calls the strongest case yet made for the view that animals have the same basic moral rights as humans do, ultimately fails. According to Warren, the notion of "inherent value" upon which Regan relies is too obscure to serve as the foundation of rights. Furthermore, she says, Regan's view, according to which every animal either has inherent value and thus the same basic rights as humans, or has no inherent value and thus none of the rights humans do, draws an implausible division. Rather, on the view Warren favors, animals have some rights that are worth taking seriously but human beings have more in virtue of being rational. Rationality matters, Warren believes, because only rational beings can negotiate with each other and make mutual compromises to promote harmonious living.

Tom Regan has produced what is perhaps the definitive defense of the view that the basic moral rights of at least some non-human animals are in no way inferior to our own. In *The Case for Animal Rights*, he argues that all nor-

Mary Anne Warren, "Difficulties with the Strong Animal Rights Position," *Between the Species*, vol. 2, Fall 1987, pp. 163–73. Copyright © 1987 by *Between the Species*. Reproduced by permission of the publisher and the author.

mal mammals over a year of age have the same basic moral rights. Non-human mammals have essentially the same right not to be harmed or killed as we do. I shall call this "the strong animal rights position," although it is weaker than the claims made by some animal liberationists in that it ascribes rights to only some sentient animals.

I will argue that Regan's case for the strong animal rights position is unpersuasive and that this position entails consequences which a reasonable person cannot accept. I do not deny that some non-human animals have moral rights; indeed, I would extend the scope of the rights claim to include all sentient animals, that is, all those capable of having experiences, including experiences of pleasure or satisfaction and pain, suffering, or frustration. However, I do not think that the moral rights of most non-human animals are identical in strength to those of persons. The rights of most non-human animals may be overridden in circumstances which would not justify overriding the rights of persons. There are, for instance, compelling realities which sometimes require that we kill animals for reasons which could not justify the killing of persons. I will call this view "the weak animal rights" position, even though it ascribes rights to a wider range of animals than does the strong animal rights position. . . .

The Mystery of Inherent Value

Inherent value is a key concept in Regan's theory. It is the bridge between the plausible claim that all normal, mature mammals—human or otherwise—are subjects-of-a-life and the more debatable claim that they all have basic moral rights of the same strength. But it is a highly obscure concept, and its obscurity makes it ill-suited to play this crucial role.

Inherent value is defined almost entirely in negative terms. It is not dependent upon the value which either the inherently valuable individual or anyone else may place upon that individual's life or experiences. It is not (necessarily) a function of sentience or any other mental capacity, because, Regan says, some entities which are not sentient (e.g., trees, rivers, or rocks) may, nevertheless, have inherent value. It cannot attach to anything other than an individual; species, eco-systems, and the like cannot have inherent value.

These are some of the things which inherent value is not. But what is it? Unfortunately, we are not told. Inherent value appears as a mysterious non-natural property which we must take on faith. Regan says that it is a *postulate* that subjects-of-a-life have inherent value, a postulate justified by the fact that it avoids certain absurdities which he thinks follow from a purely utilitarian theory. But why is the postulate that *subjects-of-a-life* have inherent value? If the inherent value of a being is completely independent of the value that it or anyone else places upon its experiences, then why does the fact that it has certain sorts of experiences constitute evidence that it has inherent value? If the reason is that subjects-of-a-life have an existence which can go better or worse for them, then why isn't the appropriate conclusion that all sentient beings have inherent value, since they would all seem to meet that condition? Sentient but mentally unsophisticated beings may have a less extensive range of possible satisfactions and frustrations, but why should it follow that they have—or may have—no inherent value at all?

In the absence of a positive account of inherent value, it is also difficult to grasp the connection between being inherently valuable and having moral rights. Intuitively, it seems that value is one thing, and rights are another. It does not seem incoherent to say that some things (e.g., mountains, rivers, redwood trees) are inherently valuable and yet are not the sorts of things which can have moral rights. Nor does it seem incoherent to ascribe inherent value to some things which are not individuals, e.g., plant or animal species, though it may well be incoherent to ascribe moral rights to such things.

In short, the concept of inherent value seems to create at least as many problems as it solves. If inherent value is based on some natural property, then why not try to identify that property and explain its moral significance, without appealing to inherent value? And if it is not based on any natural property, then why should we believe in it? That it may enable us to avoid some of the problems faced by the utilitarian is not a sufficient reason, if it creates other problems which are just as serious.

Is There a Sharp Line?

Perhaps the most serious problems are those that arise when we try to apply the strong animal rights position to animals other than normal, mature mammals. Regan's theory requires us to divide all living things into two categories: those which have the same inherent value and the same basic moral rights that we do, and those which have no inherent value and presumably no moral rights. But wherever we try to draw the line, such a sharp division is implausible.

It would surely be arbitrary to draw such a sharp line between normal, mature mammals and all other living things. Some birds (e.g., crows, magpies, parrots, mynahs) appear to be just as mentally sophisticated as most mammals and thus are equally strong candidates for inclusion under the subject-of-a-life criterion. Regan is not in fact advocating that we draw the line here. His claim is only that normal, mature mammals are clear cases, while other cases are less clear. Yet, on his theory, there must be such a sharp line *somewhere*, since there are no degrees of inherent value. But why should we believe that there is a sharp line between creatures that are subjects-of-a-life and creatures that are not? Isn't it more likely that "subjecthood" comes in degrees, that some creatures have only a little self-awareness, and only a little capacity to anticipate the future, while some have a little more, and some a good deal more?

Should we, for instance, regard fish, amphibians, and

reptiles as subjects-of-a-life? A simple yes-or-no answer seems inadequate. On the one hand, some of their behavior is difficult to explain without the assumption that they have sensations, beliefs, desires, emotions, and memories; on the other hand, they do not seem to exhibit very much self-awareness or very much conscious anticipation of future events. Do they have enough mental sophistication to count as subjects-of-a-life? Exactly how much is enough?

Unclear Cases

It is still more unclear what we should say about insects, spiders, octopi, and other invertebrate animals which have brains and sensory organs but whose minds (if they have minds) are even more alien to us than those of fish or reptiles. Such creatures are probably sentient. Some people doubt that they can feel pain, since they lack certain neurological structures which are crucial to the processing of pain impulses in vertebrate animals. But this argument is inconclusive, since their nervous systems might process pain in ways different from ours. When injured, they sometimes act as if they are in pain. On evolutionary grounds, it seems unlikely that highly mobile creatures with complex sensory systems would not have developed a capacity for pain (and pleasure), since such a capacity has obvious survival value. It must, however, be admitted that we do not *know* whether spiders can feel pain (or something very like it), let alone whether they have emotions, memories, beliefs, desires, self-awareness, or a sense of the future.

Even more mysterious are the mental capacities (if any) of mobile microfauna. The brisk and efficient way that paramecia move about in their incessant search for food *might* indicate some kind of sentience, in spite of their lack of eyes, ears, brains, and other organs associated with sentience in more complex organisms. It is conceivable—though not very probable—that they, too, are subjects-of-a-life.

The existence of a few unclear cases need not pose a serious problem for a moral theory, but in this case, the unclear cases constitute most of those with which an adequate theory of animal rights would need to deal. The subject-of-a-life criterion can provide us with little or no moral guidance in our interactions with the vast majority of animals. That might be acceptable if it could be supplemented with additional principles which would provide such guidance. However, the radical dualism of the theory precludes supplementing it in this way. We are forced to say that either a spider has the same right to life as you and I do, or it has no right to life whatever—and that only the gods know which of these alternatives is true.

Regan's suggestion for dealing with such unclear cases is to apply the "benefit of the doubt" principle. That is, when dealing with beings that may or may not be subjects-of-a-life, we should act as if they are. But if we try to apply this principle to the entire range of doubtful cases, we will find ourselves with moral obligations which we cannot possibly fulfill. In many climates, it is virtually impossible to live without swatting mosquitoes and exterminating cockroaches, and not all of us can afford to hire someone to sweep the path before we walk, in order to make sure that we do not step on ants. Thus, we are still faced with the daunting task of drawing a sharp line somewhere on the continuum of life forms—this time, a line demarcating the limits of the benefit of the doubt principle.

The weak animal rights theory provides a more plausible way of dealing with this range of cases, in that it allows the rights of animals of different kinds to vary in strength. . . .

Why Rationality Matters

How can we justify regarding the rights of persons as generally stronger than those of sentient beings which are not persons? There are a plethora of bad justifications, based on religious premises or false or unprovable claims about the differences between human and non-human nature. But there is one difference which has a clear moral relevance: people are at least sometimes capable of being moved to action or inaction by the force of reasoned argument. Rationality rests upon other mental capacities, notably those which Regan cites as criteria for being a subject-of-a-life. We share these capacities with many other animals. But it is not just because we are subjects-of-a-life that we are both able and morally compelled to recognize one another as beings with equal basic moral rights. It is also because we are able to "listen to reason" in order to settle our conflicts and cooperate in shared projects. This capacity, unlike the others, may require something like a human language.

Why is rationality morally relevant? It does not make us "better" than other animals or more "perfect." It does not even automatically make us more intelligent. (Bad reasoning reduces our effective intelligence rather than increasing it.) But it is morally relevant insofar as it provides greater possibilities for cooperation and for the nonviolent resolution of problems. It also makes us more dangerous than non-rational beings can ever be. Because we are potentially more dangerous and less predictable than wolves, we need an articulated system of morality to regulate our conduct. Any human morality, to be workable in the long run, must recognize the equal moral status of all persons, whether through the postulate of equal basic moral rights or in some other way. The recognition of the moral equality of other persons is the price we must each pay for their recognition of our moral equality. Without this mutual recognition of moral equality, human society can exist only in a state of chronic and bitter conflict. The war between the sexes will persist so long as there is sexism and male domination; racial conflict will never be eliminated so long as there are racist laws and practices. But, to the extent that we achieve a mutual recognition of equality, we can hope to live together, perhaps as peacefully as wolves, achieving (in part) through explicit moral principles what they do not seem to need explicit moral principles to achieve.

Why not extend this recognition of moral equality to other creatures, even though they cannot do the same for us? The answer is that we cannot. Because we cannot reason with most non-human animals, we cannot always solve the problems which they may cause without harming them—although we are always obligated to try. We cannot negotiate a treaty with the feral cats and foxes, requiring them to stop preying on endangered native species in return for suitable concessions on our part. If rats invade our houses . . . we cannot reason with them, hoping to persuade them of the injustice they do us. We can only attempt to get rid of them. [Bonnie Steinbock, "Speciesism and the Idea of Equality," *Philosophy*, vol. 53, no. 204 (April 1978): 247–56.

Aristotle was not wrong in claiming that the capacity to alter one's behavior on the basis of reasoned argument is relevant to the full moral status which he accorded to free men. Of course, he was wrong in his other premise, that women and slaves by their nature cannot reason well enough to function as autonomous moral agents. Had that premise been true, so would his conclusion that women and slaves are not quite the moral equals of free men. In the case of most non-human animals, the corresponding premise is true. If, on the other hand, there are animals with whom we can (learn to) reason, then we are obligated to do this and to regard them as our moral equals.

Thus, to distinguish between the rights of persons and those of most other animals on the grounds that only people can alter their behavior on the basis of reasoned argument does not commit us to a perfectionist theory of the sort Aristotle endorsed. There is no excuse for refusing to recognize the moral equality of some people on the grounds that we don't regard them as quite as rational as we are, since it is perfectly clear that most people can reason well enough to determine how to act so as to respect the basic rights of others (if they choose to), and that is enough for moral equality.

But what about people who are clearly not rational? It is often argued that sophisticated mental capacities such as rationality cannot be essential for the possession of equal basic moral rights, since nearly everyone agrees that human infants and mentally incompetent persons have such rights, even though they may lack those sophisticated mental capacities. But this argument is inconclusive, because there are powerful practical and emotional reasons for protecting non-rational human beings, reasons which are absent in the case of most non-human animals. Infancy and mental incompetence are human conditions which all of us either have experienced or are likely to experience at some time. We also protect babies and mentally incompetent people because we care for them. We don't normally care for animals in the same way, and when we do—e.g., in the case of much-loved pets—we may regard them as having special rights by virtue of their relationship to us. We protect them not only for their sake but also for our own, lest we be hurt by harm done to them. Regan holds that such "side-effects" are irrelevant to moral rights, and perhaps they are. But in ordinary usage, there is no sharp line between moral rights and those moral protections which are not rights. The extension of strong moral protections to infants and the mentally impaired in no way proves that non-human animals have the same basic moral rights as people.

Animals Feel Pleasure and Pain

DAVID DeGRAZIA

One of the key claims made by most proponents of animal rights is that animals have the capacity to feel pain and pleasure and that this means they have a right to be left alone. In the following excerpt from an introductory text on animal rights, philosopher David DeGrazia considers the evidence for this claim. According to DeGrazia, in deciding whether some particular animal feels pleasure and pain, we have three main sources of information. First is behavior: Does the animal demonstrate the right kind of behavior in the right situations? Second is physiology: Are there physiological similarities between the animal and human beings, or does the animal's nervous system have the kind of biological complexity we believe is associated with pain? Third is evolutionary considerations: Would having conscious experience of pleasure and pain help explain why the animal has evolved? After considering the evidence, DeGrazia concludes that most animals, and probably all vertebrates, can feel pain and pleasure.

Cornered in the garage, the trembling racoon slowly backs up, focusing her eyes on the man who approaches with broom in hand. The man, who wants to chase the racoon out of the garage, sees the animal's behaviour as fearful. Her leg caught in a steel trap that has cut deep into the skin, a fox struggles for hours to free herself, to no avail, before slowly chewing off her leg and separating herself from the trap. A passerby who sees the fox just as she tears away from the trap—and her leg—perceives her as experiencing great pain and suffering. Staying at a kennel for the first time, as his human companion family takes a trip out of town, a dog is hypervigilant and jumpy, and urinates on the floor. The kennel worker assumes that the dog is anxious in this unfamiliar setting.

The attributions of fear to the racoon, pain and suffering to the fox, and even anxiety to the dog are natural enough, but are they well-grounded? Does available evidence support such interpretations of animals' behaviour? More generally, what sorts of mental lives do animals have? ... [This article's] central claim is that a wide range of animals, including most or all vertebrates and probably some invertebrates, possess a rich variety of feelings. Before going to the evidence, though, we should clarify a few key terms.

Some Basic Concepts

To have any mental states or mental life at all, a being must have some *awareness* or *consciousness.* But what is awareness? We may elucidate the term by reference to other familiar terms and by use of examples.

A human or animal is aware at a particular time if he or she is having any subjective experiences at that time. Such experiences include all states of consciousness when we are awake and even those confused modes of thinking and feeling known as dream experiences. A closely related concept is that of *sentience*—the capacity to have *feelings.* Feelings, in turn, include both *felt sensations*, such as pain and nausea, and *emotional states*, such as fear and joy. All sentient beings have states of awareness. For example, presumably all sentient animals can feel at least painful and pleasant sensations.

It is important to distinguish awareness from *nociception.* Nociception, the first event in a sequence that often involves pain, is the detection of potentially noxious, or tissue-damaging, stimuli by specialized neural end-organs—nociceptors—which fire impulses along axons (nerve fibres that serve as pathways). Such stimuli include cutting, pressure, pricking, heat, cold, inflammation of tissues, and muscle spasms. While nociception itself is not a state of awareness or consciousness, it often occurs together with such states, typically pain. . . .

While there is no perfect definition of 'awareness', our experience and common sense are sufficient to understand this basic concept. Whenever we are awake or dreaming, we experience subjective states; and we know that, in certain sleeping states and under general anaesthesia, we have no such subjective states. As we will see, empirical evidence strongly supports the common-sense judgement that many animals also have states of awareness, even if their consciousness is less complex, reflective, and language-laden than human consciousness typically is.

Evidence for Pain and Other Sensations in Animals

Although nearly everyone believes that many animals experience pain, a responsible discussion of animal mentality must consider whether evidence supports this or any other attribution. But here, as with other mental states, we need a working definition to clarify what we are looking for. Our own experience—or phenomenology—of pain combined with scientific study of the phenomenon supports roughly this understanding: *pain is an unpleasant or aversive sensory experience typically associated with actual or potential tissue damage.* (This definition doesn't cover 'emotional pain', a figurative extension of the most literal sense of 'pain'; 'suffering' is often an apt and more literal substitute for 'emotional pain'.)

Now, when we ask whether a particular sort of creature experiences a type of mental state, four kinds of evidence are relevant. First, human phenomenology helps to categorize mental states and informs us of what they feel like.

From this starting-point, which can help to establish a working definition, we can argue that non-human animals have a particular mental state on the strength of three other sources of information: animals' behaviour in context, their physiology, and functional-evolutionary considerations. The latter address the adaptive value of a type of mental state for a specific kind of creature living in a particular environmental niche.

Let us consider such evidence in connection with pain. Certainly, animals often behave as if in pain. Any of these three types of behaviour is at least somewhat suggestive of pain: (1) avoiding or escaping a noxious stimulus (for example, withdrawing a paw from a sharp object); (2) getting assistance (for example, crying out) after a noxious event; and (3) limiting the use of an overworked or injured body part to permit rest and healing (for example, immobilizing a pulled muscle and favouring another limb). The vast majority of animals, including insects, exhibit behaviours of type (1), though in some animals such behaviours may be due to nociception without pain or some similar type of non-conscious response to stimuli. Vertebrates and perhaps some invertebrates also display behaviours of type (3). Type (2), which may be relevant only to comparatively social animals, is common among mammals and birds. Evidence of learning and adaptation to novel circumstances strengthen the claim that behaviours of any of these three types indicate pain—and therefore sentience. Such evidence is found in the case of vertebrates and at least some invertebrate species such as octopuses and squid.

Turning now to physiological evidence for animal pain, there is extensive commonality across vertebrate species of the biological machinery apparently required for pain. Pain is associated with certain physiological changes, including measurable nerve impulses in specific pathways and metabolic and electrical activity in particular parts of the brain. In turn, these events elicit other physiological responses such as changes in the sympathetic adrenomedullary system and the hypothalamic-pituitary-adrenocortical system. Not only are the neurophysiology and neuroanatomy of pain quite similar in these animals; they also share the biological mechanisms for modulating pain, such as endogenous opiates. Moreover, anaesthesia and analgesia control what is apparently pain in all vertebrates and some invertebrates. Indeed, if animals were not significantly analogous to humans in the capacity for pain and other aversive mental states, it would be senseless to use animals as models for the study of these states in humans.

An Evolutionary Argument

Consideration of pain's function in the context of evolutionary theory constitutes another form of evidence for animal pain. The biological function of pain is evidently (1) to provide an organism information about where tissue damage may occur, is occurring, or has occurred and (2) to motivate responses that are likely to avoid or minimize damage, such as rapid limb movement away from a noxious stimulus or immobilizing muscles to permit recuperation. Pain's unpleasantness provides the motivation for adaptive, life-preserving responses.

Then again, one might reply, perhaps nociception or some similar event—without pain or any conscious awareness— would function equally well to keep animals out of harm's way, in which case functional-evolutionary arguments might not support the case for animal pain. But evolution tends to preserve successful biological systems. And rather than spontaneously producing new creatures well-suited for particular niches, with no 'design constraints', evolution operates within the limits of the genetic endowment and anatomical systems inherited from evolutionary forebears. Now we know that in humans the ability to feel pain is important for functioning and survival. Humans with significantly impaired or no ability to feel pain, such as people with anaesthetic leprosy, are in danger of not surviving without extraordinary attention. The fact that neural structures similar to those that produce our consciousness are found in vertebrates—in combination with their pain behaviour—suggests that pain has a similar function for them and that natural selection has preserved the capacity for pain throughout the evolution of at least the vertebrates.

However, in all but the most 'advanced' invertebrates, such as octopuses and squids, there is genuine uncertainty regarding pain and, more generally, sentience. For example, the impressively complex behaviour of some insects, such as ants and bees, may seem to suggest sentience; one might take apparent pain behaviour in all insects—avoiding or escaping noxious stimuli—as strong evidence of pain in these creatures. Then again, some insect behaviour, such as continuing normal behaviour after injury or loss of body parts, and not taking weight off injured limbs, strongly suggests lack of sentience. Moreover, insects have extremely primitive nervous systems by comparison to vertebrates. Finally, with their short life spans and modest learning needs, insects might derive little advantage from conscious states such as pain; a startle reflex might suffice to enable escape from danger in most circumstances. Thus, the evidence available today is too indeterminate to justify confidently drawing the line between sentient and non-sentient animals in any specific place, although it is virtually certain that some invertebrates, such as amoebas, are non-sentient.

While there is much uncertainty regarding the possible sentience of invertebrates, as we have seen, evidence overwhelmingly supports the proposition that many animals, apparently including all vertebrates, can feel pain. But there is little doubt that animals who can feel pain can also feel pleasure—at least in the form of *pleasant sensations.* (That animals also experience pleasant *emotions* would require further arguments.) We may say the same of *bodily discomfort*, an unpleasant sensation distinct from pain. But here we cannot explore precise definitions or specific evidence for these mental states.

Evidence for Distress, Fear, Anxiety, and Suffering

While pain is sensory and therefore associated with specific body parts, distress, fear, anxiety, and suffering are emotional and therefore associated with the entire subject who experiences them. Before considering specific evidence for the occurrence of these states in animals, let us clarify the concepts themselves.

We may start with suffering, which has a sort of umbrella relationship to the others. Note that suffering differs from pain since either can occur without the other. If I pinch my hand, I have pain without suffering, whereas someone having a panic attack suffers without pain. Nor does suffering equal distress: if you are only mildly distressed due to a deadline, you do not suffer. *Suffering is a highly unpleasant emotional state associated with more-than-minimal pain or distress.* Since suffering is defined in terms of pain and distress, the evidence for suffering is the same as that for pain or distress—or high degrees thereof. Pain we discussed earlier.

Distress is a typically unpleasant emotional response to the perception of environmental challenges or to equilibrium-disrupting internal stimuli. It can be caused by such diverse phenomena as the sight of approaching predators, the belief that one will fail, or diarrhoea. Distress can take the form of various more specific mental states, such as fear, anxiety, frustration, and boredom. While a thorough exploration of distress would investigate all such related mental states, here we will consider just fear and anxiety.

Fear motivates focused responses to perceived dangers and preparation for future responses. While perhaps mild fear can be pleasant, as with skiing, fear tends to be unpleasant. *Fear is a typically unpleasant emotional response to a perceived danger (usually in the immediate environment), a response that focuses attention to facilitate protective action.* By contrast, anxiety involves a generalized, as opposed to focused, state of heightened arousal and attention to the environment. It usually immobilizes our mental resources and inhibits our action, so we can attend to our environment until we have determined how to respond to any challenges that may arise. While fear and anxiety are closely related, anxiety serves especially well in unfamiliar situations, explaining why it is less focused than fear. Moreover, at least with humans, often the object of anxiety is possible damage to one's self-image. *Anxiety is a typically unpleasant emotional response to a perceived threat to one's physical or psychological well-being, a response that generally inhibits action and involves heightened arousal and attention to the environment.* Commonsensically, fear and anxiety have similar protective functions in complementary settings. For example, a cat may be anxious in the novel setting of a veterinarian's waiting room. In her second visit there, she may feel fear due to remembering a painful shot she received during the previous visit. But let us move beyond commonsense claims to rigorous evidence.

Similarities to Humans

Consider the evidence for anxiety, which of the mental states under discussion is most likely to inspire scepticism. First, typical behavioural and physiological features of human anxiety are also found in many animals in circumstances that are likely to make animals anxious, if any would: (1) autonomic hyperactivity—pounding heart, sweating, increased pulse rate and respiration, etc.; (2) motor tension, as seen in jumpiness; (3) inhibition of normal behaviours in novel situations; and (4) hyperattentiveness, as seen in visual scanning. Consistent with the definition of anxiety, these findings add up to strong behavioural evidence and some physiological evidence for anxiety in animals. In addition, we have already seen the adaptive value, or evolutionary function, of anxiety; it permits a creature to inhibit action and attend carefully to the environment in preparation for protective action.

Further, human anxiety and some mental states in animals—which we infer to be anxiety—are mediated in similar ways by certain drugs that cause similar neurophysiological and neurochemical changes. In one kind of test, for example, randomly punishing thirsty rats causes reduced drinking, the inhibition of a normal behaviour. But giving the rats an anti-anxiety drug restores drinking to more normal rates. Another kind of test places animals in novel settings such as brightly lit open spaces. Animals who are given anti-anxiety drugs beforehand exhibit what is apparently less anxious behaviour than animals who are not given these drugs. Moreover, when drugs that *induce* anxiety in humans are given to animal subjects, they display the behaviours and physiological responses associated with anxiety.

Since most of the subjects of these latter studies were mammals, the following findings are of special interest. Scientists have long known that benzodiazepine receptors, which in humans are the substrate for nearly all known anti-anxiety agents, are also found in mammals. More recent research demonstrated that none of the five invertebrates tested, nor the one cartilaginous fish (an animal at the border between vertebrates and invertebrates), had these receptors. Yet all the other species examined—including three species of birds, a lizard, frog, and turtle, and three species of bony fishes—had such receptors, providing some additional evidence that at least most vertebrates can experience anxiety.

While the available evidence, taken together, supports this conclusion, it does not imply that human anxiety and animal anxiety are qualitatively similar beyond a common unpleasantness and heightened arousal and attention. Undoubtedly, the language-laden complexity of human thought produces anxious experiences very different from those of animals. The present claim is that animals representing a wide range of species are capable of having anxious states, as captured in our definition of 'anxiety'.

Given the close relationship between anxiety and fear, as

explained above, one would expect that animals capable of being anxious are also capable of being afraid. Supporting this common-sense judgement is the fact that all vertebrates have autonomic-nervous and limbic systems, which contain the basic substrates of fear and anxiety. And, of course, such animals often behave as if in fear—a state that has great adaptive value from an evolutionary standpoint.

But if certain animals can experience fear and anxiety—which are forms of distress—there is no further question of whether they can experience distress. Can they suffer, though? Suffering, again, is a highly unpleasant emotional state associated with more-than-minimal pain or distress. We have already argued that vertebrates can experience pain and distress, But if some animals can experience these states only *minimally*—that is, not very intensely—that would imply that they cannot suffer. It is unclear what would count as evidence that certain animals could have only minimal pain and distress, beyond the general speculation that the most primitive sentient creatures have dim mental lives. In any case, since apparently all vertebrates and at least some invertebrates are sentient, I recommend the tentative assumption that at least *most* vertebrates can suffer.

Animal Rights Are Easy to Recognize but Hard to Respect

ROBERT WRIGHT

In the following article, originally published in the news weekly New Republic, *columnist Robert Wright reflects on the development of animal rights theory. According to Wright, in the process of researching animal rights he slowly became convinced of the philosophical soundness of the position. Wright argues that if we accept it is wrong to harm animals gratuitously (by, for example, beating or torturing them), we are led inexorably toward the view that animals have rights. Wright notes, however, that there are two main challenges to broad public acceptance of animal rights. The first is that animals, unlike oppressed racial minorities or women, cannot advocate on their own behalf. The second is that human beings may not be able, or willing, to identify with animals and in so doing feel compassion for their situation.*

I recently interviewed several animal rights activists in hopes that they would say some amusing, crazy-sounding things that might liven up this article. More often than not I was disappointed. They would come close to making unreservedly extremist pronouncements but then step back from the brink, leaving me with a quote that was merely provocative. For example, Ingrid Newkirk, co-founder of People for the Ethical Treatment of Animals (PETA), seemed on the verge of conceding that Frank Perdue is no better than Adolf Hitler—a proposition that technically follows from her premise that animals possess the moral status of humans (and from references in animal rights literature to the ongoing "animal holocaust"). But she wouldn't go all the way. "He's the animals' Hitler, I'll give you that," she said. "If you were a chicken . . . you wouldn't think he was Mother Teresa." The other co-founder of PETA, Alex Pacheco, was not much more helpful. "You and I are equal to the lobsters when it comes to being boiled alive," he said, raising my hopes. But, he added, "I don't mean I couldn't decide which one to throw in, myself or the lobster."

The biggest disappointment was a woman who went by the pseudonym "Helen." She was a member of the Animal Liberation Front [ALF], a shadowy group that goes around breaking into scientific laboratories, documenting the conditions therein, and sometimes burning down the labs (minus the animals, which are typically "liberated"—taken somewhere else—in the process). Given all the intrigue involved in interviewing "Helen"—I had to "put out the word" that I wanted to talk with an ALF member, and when she called she always used a streetside phone booth and never left a number—I expected a rich encounter. This hope grew when I found out that she had participated in a recent lab-burning at the University of Arizona. But as professed arsonists go, Helen seemed like a very nice and fairly reasonable person. She was a combination of earnest moral anguish ("For the most part, people just aren't aware of how much suffering and death goes into what they eat and wear. . . . Most people just literally don't know") and crisp professionalism ("Whether I have any animosity toward [laboratory researchers] is irrelevant. . . . I just do everything I can to move them into a different job category"). And though her reverence for life may strike you as creepy—she picks up spiders off the floor and moves them outdoors, rather than squash them—it is not unbounded. She assured me that if termites were destroying her home, she would call an exterminator.

One reason for this general failure to gather satisfactorily extremist quotes is that animal rights activists have become more media-savvy, developing a surer sense for when they are being baited. But another reason is my own failure to find their ideas extremist. Slowly I seem to be getting drawn into the logic of animal rights. I still eat meat, wear a leather belt, and support the use of animals in important scientific research. But not without a certain amount of cognitive dissonance.

A Slippery Slope

The animal rights movement, which has mushroomed during the past decade, most conspicuously in the growth of PETA (membership around 300,000), is distinguished from the animal welfare movement, as represented by, for example, the Humane Society of the United States. Animal *welfare* activists don't necessarily claim that animals are the moral equivalent of humans, just that animals' feelings deserve some consideration; we shouldn't needlessly hurt them—with pointless experimentation, say, or by making fur coats. And just about every thinking person, if pressed, will agree that animal welfare is a legitimate idea. Hardly anyone believes in kicking dogs.

But the truth is that animal welfare is just the top of a slippery slope that leads to animal rights. Once you buy the premise that animals can experience pain and pleasure, and that their welfare therefore deserves *some* consideration, you're on the road to comparing yourself with a lobster. There may be some exit ramps along the way—plausible places to separate welfare from rights—but I can't find any. And if you don't manage to find one, you wind up not only with a rather more sanguine view of animal rights but also with a more cynical view of the concept of human rights and its historical evolution.

None of this is to say that a few minutes of philosophical reflection will lead you to start wearing dumpling-shaped fake-leather shoes, sporting a "Meat is Murder" button, or referring to your pet dog as your "companion animal." The stereotype about the people who do these things—that they're ill at ease in human society, even downright antagonistic toward other humans—is generally wrong, but the stereotype that they're, well, *different* from most people is not. These are dyed-in-the-wool activists, and if they weren't throwing themselves into this cause, they would probably be throwing themselves into some other cause. (Pacheco, for example, had originally planned to become a priest.) Moreover, very few of them were converted to the movement solely or mainly via philosophy. Many will say they were critically influenced by the book *Animal Liberation* (1975), written by the Australian ethicist Peter Singer, but reading Singer was for most of them merely a ratifying experience, a seal of philosophical approval for their intuitive revulsion at animal suffering. Pacheco received a copy of the book the same week he got grossed out while touring a Canadian slaughterhouse. He later gave a copy to Newkirk, who was then chief of Animal Disease Control for the District of Columbia. Around that time she spent a day trying to rescue some starving, neglected horses that were locked in their stalls and mired in mud. That's when it hit her: "It didn't make sense. I had spent the whole day trying to get some starving horses out of a stall and here I was going home to eat some other animal." This gut perception is a recurring theme, as crystallized by Helen: "I just realized that if I wouldn't eat my dog, why should I eat a cow?"

Why Sentience Matters

Good question. And implicit in it is the core of the case for animal rights: the modest claim—not disputed by anyone who has ever owned a dog or cat, so far as I know—that animals are sentient beings, capable of pleasure and pain. People who would confine natural rights to humans commonly talk about the things we have that animals don't—

complex language, sophisticated reasoning, a highly evolved culture. But none of these is important, for moral purposes, in the way that sheer sentience is.

One way to appreciate this is through a simple thought experiment. Suppose there's a planet populated by organisms that look and act exactly like humans. They walk, talk, flirt, go to law school, blush in response to embarrassing comments, and discuss their impending deaths in glum tones. Now suppose it turns out they're automatons, made out of silicon chips—or even made out of flesh and blood. The important thing is that all their behavior—their blushing, their discussion of death—is entirely a product of the physical circuitry inside their heads and isn't accompanied by any subjective experience; they can't feel pain, pleasure, or anything else. In other words (to use the terminology of [the philosopher] Thomas Nagel), it isn't like anything to be them.

Is there anything particularly immoral about slapping one of them in the face? Most everyone would say: obviously not, since it doesn't hurt. How about killing one of them? Again, no; their death doesn't preclude their future experience of happiness, as with real live humans, or cause any pain for friends and relatives. There is no apparent reason to bestow any moral status whatsoever on these creatures, much less the exalted status that the human species now enjoys. They have powerful brains, complex language, and high culture, but none of this makes them significant.

Now rearrange the variables: subtract all these attributes and add sentience. In other words, take all the robots off the planet and populate it with non-human animals: chimps, armadillos, dogs, etc. Is there anything immoral about gratuitously hurting or killing one of these? Do they have individual rights? Most people would answer yes to the first question, and some would answer yes to the second. But the main point is that few people would quickly and easily say "no" to either, because these are harder questions than the robot question. Sentience lies at the core of our moral thinking, and language, intelligence, etc., lie nearer the periphery. Sentience seems definitely a necessary and arguably a sufficient condition for the possession of high moral status (experiments 1 and 2, respectively), whereas the other attributes are arguably necessary but definitely not sufficient (experiments 2 and 1, respectively).

The best way to get a better fix on exactly which traits are prerequisites for moral status is simply to try to explain why they *should* be. Take sentience first. We all agree from personal experience that pain is a bad thing, that no one should have the right to inflict it on us, and consistency (part of any moral system) dictates that we agree not to inflict it on anyone else. Makes sense. But now try to say something comparably compelling about why great reasoning ability or complex language are crucial to moral status. Also, try to do the same with self-consciousness—our awareness of our own existence. (This is another uniquely human attribute commonly invoked in these discussions, but we couldn't isolate it in experiment 1 above because an organism can't have it without having sentience.)

Unsuccessful Arguments

If you accept this challenge, you'll almost certainly go down one of two paths, neither of which will get you very far. First, you may try to establish that self-consciousness, complex language, etc., are the hallmarks of "spirit," the possession of which places us in some special category. This is a perfectly fine thing to believe, but it's hard to *argue* for. It depends much more on religious conviction than on any plausible line of reasoning.

The second path people take in asserting the moral significance of uniquely human attributes is even less successful, because it leads to a booby trap. This is the argument that self-consciousness and reason and language give humans a dimension of suffering that mere animals lack: because we can anticipate pain and death; and because we know that death will represent the end of our consciousness forever; and because we recognize that threats to one citizen may represent a threat to us all—because of all this, the protection of human rights is essential to everyone's peace of mind; the torture or murder of anyone in town, as conveyed to the public via language and then reflected upon at length, makes everyone tremendously fearful. So a robust conception of individual rights is essential for the welfare of a human society in a way that it isn't for, say, the welfare of a chicken society.

Sounds nice, but it amounts to philosophical surrender. To rely completely on this argument is to concede that language, reason, and self-consciousness are morally important *only* to the extent that they magnify suffering or happiness. Pain and pleasure, in other words, are the currency of moral assessment. The several uniquely human attributes may revaluate the currency, but the currency possesses some value with or without them. And many, if not all, nonhuman animals seem to possess the currency in some quantity. So unless you can come up with a nonarbitrary reason for saying that their particular quantities are worthless while our particular quantities are precious, you have to start thinking about animals in a whole new light. This explains why Peter Singer, in *Animal Liberation*, readily admits that the human brain is unique in its ability to thus compound suffering.

Once the jaws of this philosophical trap have closed on the opponents of animal rights, no amount of struggling can free them. Let them insist that language, reason, and self-consciousness *immensely* raise the moral stakes for humans. Let them add, even, that our sheer neurological complexity makes us experience raw pain more profoundly than, say, dogs or even mice do. Grant them, in other words, that in the grand utilitarian calculus, one day of solid suffering by a single human equals one day's suffering by 10,000 laboratory rats. Grant them all of this, and they still lose, because the point is that animals have now been *admitted* to the utilitarian calculus. If it is immoral, as we all believe it is, to walk up to a stranger and inflict 1/10,000 of one day's suffering (nine seconds' worth), then it is equally immoral to walk up and inflict one day's suffering on a single laboratory rat.

Actually, granting animals utilitarian value doesn't technically mean you have to extend individual rights to them. As far as sheer philosophical consistency goes, you can equally well take rights away from humans. You can say: sure, it makes sense to kill 100 baboons to save the life of one human, but it also makes sense to kill a human to save the life of 100 baboons. Whatever you say, though, you have to go one way or the other, letting such equations work either in both directions or in neither. Unless you can create a moral ratchet called "human rights"—and I don't see any way to do it—you have to choose between a planet on which every sentient creature has rights and a planet on which none does.

And of course if no creature on earth has rights, then it can make sense to kill a human not just for the sake of 100 baboons, but for the sake of two humans—or just in the name of the greater good. In other words, the logic used by animal rights activists turns out to play into the hands of the Adolf Hitlers of the world no less than the Albert Schweitzers. In *Darkness at Noon*, when Ivanov describes Stalin's rule as belonging to the school of "vivisection morality," Arthur Koestler is onto something more than good allegory.

Disturbing Images

Before figuring out whether to follow this logic toward vegetarianism or totalitarianism, let's remove it from the realm of abstraction. Spending an evening watching videotapes supplied by PETA—such as *The Animals Film*, narrated by Julie Christie—is a fairly disturbing experience. This is partly because the people who made it gave it a subtle shrillness that reflects what is most annoying about the animal rights movement. There are man-on-the-street interviews conducted by an obnoxious, self-righteous inter-rogator demanding to know how people can own dogs and eat Big Macs; there is the assumption that viewers will find the late McDonald's founder Ray Kroc—a seemingly likable guy shown innocently discussing how he settled on the name "McDonald's"—abhorrent; there is a simple-minded anti-capitalist undercurrent (as if factory farmers in so-cialist countries spent their time giving foot massages to hogs); and there is grating atonal music meant to make the sight of blood more disturbing than it naturally is.

And that's plenty disturbing, thank you. Take, for exam-ple, the chickens hung by their feet from a conveyer belt that escorts them through an automatic throat slicing ma-chine—this the culmination of a life spent on the poultry equivalent of a New York subway platform at rush hour. Or consider the deep basketfuls of male chicks, struggling not to smother before they're ground into animal feed. There's also, naturally, the veal: a calf raised in a crate so small that it can't even turn around, much less walk—the better to keep the flesh tender. There are wild furry animals cut al-most in half by steel-jawed traps but still conscious. There are rabbits getting noxious chemicals sprayed in their eyes by cosmetics companies.

And these are the animals that *don't* remind you of hu-man beings. Watching these portions of *The Animals Film* is a day at the zoo compared with watching non-human pri-mates suffer. If you don't already have a strong sense of identity with chimpanzees, gorillas, and the like—if you doubt that they're capable of crude reasoning, anticipating pain, feeling and expressing deep affection for one an-other—I suggest you patronize your local zoo (or prison, as animal rights activists would have it) and then get hold of a copy of the ethologist Frans de Waal's two amazing books, *Peace-making Among Primates* and *Chimpanzee Pol-itics*. The commonly cited fact that chimps share about ninety-eight percent of our genes is misleading, to be sure; a handful of genes affecting the brain's development can make a world of difference. Still, if you can watch a toddler chimp or gorilla for long without wanting to file for adoption, you should seek professional help.

In videotapes that Helen helped steal in 1984 from the University of Pennsylvania's Head Injury Clinical Research Center, anesthetized baboons are strapped down and their heads placed in boxlike vices that are violently snapped sixty degrees sideways by a hydraulic machine. Some of the baboons have what appear to be seizures, some go limp, and none looks very happy. Some of the lab workers—as callous as you'd have to become to do their job, perhaps—stand around and make jokes about it all. It's hard to say how much scientific good came of this, because the scientist in question refuses to talk about it. But watching the tapes, you have to hope that the data were markedly more valuable than what's already available from the study of injured humans. In any event, the experiments were halted after PETA publicized the tapes (though ostensibly for sloppy lab technique, such as occasionally inadequate anesthesia, not because of the violent nature of the experiments).

There are certainly many kinds of animal research that seem justified by any reasonable utilitarian calculus. A case in point is the lab Helen helped set afire at the University of Arizona. Among the researchers whose work was destroyed in the attack is a man named Charles Sterling, who is studying a parasite that causes diarrhea in both animals and humans and kills many children in the Third World every year. There is no way fruitfully to study this parasite in, say, a cell culture, so he uses mice, infecting them with the parasite and thereby inducing a non-lethal spell of diarrhea. (The idea repeated mindlessly by so many animal rights activists—that there's almost always an equally effective non-animal approach to experimentation—is wrong.)

Sterling is one of a handful of workers in this area, and he figures, in over-the-phone, off-the-cuff calculations, that all together they cause around 10,000 to 20,000 mice-weeks of diarrheal discomfort every year. The apparently realistic goal is to find a cure for a disease that kills more than 100,000 children a year. Sounds like a good deal to me. Again, though, the hitch is that to endorse this in a philosophically impeccable way, you have to let go of the concept of human rights, at least as classically conceived.

Expanding Rights

Then again, human rights isn't what it's classically conceived as being. It isn't some divine law imparted to us from above, or some Platonic truth apprehended through the gift of reason. The idea of individual rights is simply a non-aggression pact among everyone who subscribes to it. It's a deal struck for mutual convenience.

And, actually, it's in some sense a very old deal. A few million years ago, back when human ancestors were not much smarter than chimps, they presumably abided by an implicit and crude concept of individual rights, just as chimps do. Which is to say: life within a troop of, say, fifty or sixty individuals was in practical terms sacred. (Sure, chimps occasionally murder fellow troop members, just as humans do, but this is highly aberrant behavior. Rituals that keep bluster and small-scale aggression from escalating to fatality are well-developed. And when they fail, and death occurs, an entire chimp colony may be solemn and subdued for hours or longer as if in mourning.) At the same time, these prehuman primates were presumably much like chimps in being fairly disdainful of the lives of fellow species-members who didn't belong to the troop. At some point in human history, as troops of fifty became tribes of thousands, the circle of morally protected life grew commensurately. But the circle didn't at first extend to other tribes. Indeed, wide acceptance of the idea that people of all nations have equal moral rights is quite recent.

How did it all happen? In one of Singer's later and less famous books, *The Expanding Circle* (Farrar, Straus, & Giroux, 1981), whose title refers to exactly this process, he writes as if the circle's expansion has been driven almost Platonically, by the "inherently expansionist nature of reasoning." Once people became civilized and started thinking about the logic behind the reciprocal extension of rights to one another, he says, they were on an intellectual "escalator," and there was no turning back. The idea of uniformly applied ethical strictures "emerges because of the social nature of human beings and the requirements of group living, but in the thought of reasoning beings, it takes on a logic of its own which leads to its extension beyond the bounds of the group."

This, alas, is perhaps too rosy a view. The concept of human rights has grown more inclusive largely through raw politics. Had tribes not found it in their interest to band together—sometimes to massacre other tribes—they wouldn't have had to invent the concept of inter-tribal rights. Necessity was similarly the mother of moral invention in modern societies. Had the suffragists not deftly wielded political clout, men mightn't have seen the logic of giving women the vote. Had the abolition of slavery not acquired political moment in a war that slaughtered millions, slavery might have long persisted.

Certainly in advances of this sort an important role can be played by intellectual persuasion, by sympathy, by empathy. These can fuse with political power and reinforce it. South Africa today exemplifies the mix. President F.W. de Klerk may or may not truly buy the moral logic behind his (relatively) progressive initiatives, but he definitely has felt the accompanying political pressure, ranging from international sanctions to domestic protest and unrest. On the other hand, behind those sanctions has been, among other things, some genuine empathy and some pure moral logic.

Disadvantages for Animals

The bad news for animals is twofold. First, in all of these cases—women's rights, the abolition of slavery, ending apartheid—a good part of the political momentum comes from the oppressed themselves. Progress in South Africa never would have begun if blacks there hadn't perceived their own dignity and fought for it. Second, in all of these cases, empathy for the oppressed by influential outsiders came because the outsiders could identify with the oppressed—because, after all, they're people, too. With animal rights, in contrast, (1) the oppressed can never by themselves exert leverage; and (2) the outsiders who work on their behalf, belonging as they do to a different species, must be exquisitely, imaginatively compassionate in order to be drawn to the cause. To judge by history, this is not a recipe for success. It may forever remain the case that, when it comes time to sit down and do the moral bargaining, non-human animals, unlike all past downtrodden organisms, don't have much to bring to the table.

Notwithstanding these handicaps, the animal rights movement has made progress. American fur sales are by some accounts down (perhaps more out of fear of social disapproval than out of newfound sympathy). Some cosmetics companies have stopped abusing rabbits' eyes, finding that there are gentler ways to test products. And the university panels that administer federal laboratory regulations—designed to ensure that animal experimentation is worthwhile and not needlessly cruel—are undoubtedly, in the present climate, being at least as scrupulous as they've ever been (however scrupulous that is).

Even I—never quick to bring my deeds into sync with my words—am making minor gains. I hereby vow never again to eat veal. And it's conceivable that the dovetailing of moral concerns and health fears will get me to give up all red meat, among the most (formerly) sentient kind of flesh on the market. Also: no leather couches or leather jackets in my future. Shoes, yes, couches, no; the least we can do is distinguish between the functionally valuable and the frivolous. (Which also means, of course: people who wear fur coats to advertise their social status—which is to say all people who wear fur coats—should indeed, as the Humane Society's ads have it, be ashamed of themselves.)

Finally, for what it's worth, I plan to keep intact my lifelong record of never eating pâté de foie gras, the preternaturally enlarged liver of a goose force-fed through a large tube.

But so long as I so much as eat tuna fish and support the use of primates in AIDS research, how can I still endorse the idea of human rights? How can I consider Stalin guilty of a moral crime and not just a utilitarian arithmetic error? One answer would be to admit that my allegiance to human rights isn't philosophical in the pure sense, but pragmatic; I've implicitly signed a non-aggression pact with all other humans, and Stalin violated the pact, which is immoral in this practical sense of the term. But I'd rather answer that, yes, I think moral law should be more than a deal cut among the powerful, but, no, I haven't been any more successful than the next guy in expunging all moral contradictions from my life. I'll try to do what I can.

If there is a half-decent excuse for this particular contradiction, I suppose it is that human civilization is moving in the right direction. Given where our moral thinking was 200, 500, 5,000 years ago, we're not doing badly. The expanding circle will never get as big as Singer would like, perhaps, but if it grows even slowly and fitfully, we'll be justified in taking a certain chauvinistic pride in our species.

CHAPTER 3

Animal Rights Activism

The Public Debate over Animal Experimentation

NEWSWEEK

The following article was published in the newsmagazine
Newsweek *in December 1988. It discusses the growing recognition in the United States that there are serious moral issues
involved in animal experimentation. The article describes the
conflict between scientists, who praise the benefits to humans
of such experiments, and animal rights activists, who point
out that those benefits come at the expense of great animal
suffering. The article also discusses the work of the academic
philosopher Peter Singer, demonstrating that by the mid-1980s
his ideas had begun to filter into the public imagination.*

For 14 years, Michiko Okamoto heard nothing but praise
for the medical experiments she performed on animals.
By force-feeding barbiturates to groups of cats for periods
of several weeks, then cutting off their supplies, the Cornell University pharmacologist learned a lot about the dy-
namics of addiction and withdrawal. She showed that the
moderate drug doses prescribed by physicians can, over
time, be as physically addictive as the fixes sold on the
street. And she explained why addicts die from overdoses
even after their bodies have grown tolerant of particular
drugs. Okamoto's work won numerous grants from the National Institute on Drug Abuse (NIDA) and her findings are

cited in standard medical texts. According to Keith Killam, a professor of pharmacology at the University of California, Davis, the cat experiments are "a shining, crystal example of how to do science."

Steve Siegel of Trans-Species Unlimited, a Pennsylvania-based animal-rights group, calls them "the worst of the worst." Last year Siegel's group mounted a massive campaign against Okamoto. It printed brochures describing, in her own words, how her cats would stand "trembling [and] salivating" after she suddenly stopped pumping drugs into their stomachs—how they would hiss at imagined tormentors or collapse and die "during or soon after periods of continuous convulsive activity." For four months Trans-Species' supporters picketed Okamoto's laboratory and barraged her with phone calls. Cornell and NIDA officials received more than 10,000 letters condemning the experiments.

This fall, after making a statement that was widely, if mistakenly, viewed as a promise to stop the cat studies, Cornell and Okamoto surrendered. In an unprecedented gesture, they wrote NIDA to say they would forfeit a new $530,000 three-year research grant.

It was, depending on your perspective, a moral victory for abused and innocent creatures or a defeat for science and medicine. Either way, the case of the Cornell cats was just the latest example of America's growing preoccupation with the moral status of animals. Scholars say more has been written on the subject in the past 12 years [1976–1988] than in the previous 3,000. And grassroots organizations are proliferating wildly. Just 15 years ago [1973], talk of animal welfare was pretty well confined to the humane societies. Today there are some 7,000 animal-protection groups in the United States, with combined memberships of 10 million and total budgets of some $50 million. Says Carol Burnett, spokeswoman for the Washington-based group People for the Ethical Treatment of Animals: "We're really gaining steam."

A Variety of Tactics

That's not to say everybody's riding the same train. The activists' demands range from securing better lab conditions to setting all animals free, and their tactics range from letter writing to burglary. Yet they've become a potent collective presence. Animal advocates have sponsored numerous local ballot initiatives to regulate the treatment of farm animals, or ban the use of animals in product-safety tests, or exempt school kids from mandatory dissection lessons. They've declared war on the fur industry, agitated against particular scientists, as in the Cornell case, and organized to block construction of new animal-research facilities. At Stanford University, plans for a new $18 million animal lab were held up for more than a year when the Palo Alto Humane Society opposed the project before the county board of supervisors. Construction is now under way, but the delay cost the university more than $2 million.

There has been civil disobedience, too—even violence. Just last month a woman affiliated with the animal-rights cause was arrested outside the United States Surgical Corp. in Norwalk, Conn., and charged with planting a radio-controlled pipe bomb near the company chairman's parking place. Fires and break-ins, many of them linked to the militant Animal Liberation Front, have caused millions of dollars' worth of damage at labs around the country. The fear of such incidents is fast turning research centers into bunkers. After two bomb threats and at least five attempted break-ins, officials at Emory University's Yerkes Regional Primate Research Center recently spent hundreds of thousands of dollars on new alarms and electronic locks. Other institutions, including Harvard Medical School, have taken similar steps.

In short, the debate over animal rights is forcing basic changes in the way universities, corporations and government agencies do business. More than that, it's prompting a reconsideration of mankind's place in the web of life. As the political scientist Walter Truett Anderson observes in his recent book "To Govern Evolution," the cause of animal rights is not just a passing fancy. It is a "principled attempt to redefine some of our most basic concepts about the nature of political rights and obligations."

The number of creatures used in research, education and product testing each year is indeed staggering. Though estimates run as high as 100 million, federal agencies place the total at 17 million to 22 million—a figure that includes some 50,000 cats, 61,000 primates, 180,000 dogs, 554,000 rabbits and millions of mice and rats (which fill 80 to 90 percent of the demand).

Hurting Animals to Help Humans

The killing is not without purpose; it has immense practical benefits. Animal models have advanced the study of such diseases as cancer, diabetes and alcoholism and yielded lifesaving treatments for everything from heart disease to manic-depressive illness. Vaccines developed through animal research have virtually wiped out diseases like smallpox and polio. "Every surgical technique was tried first in animals," says Frankie Trull, executive director of the Foundation for Biomedical Research. "Every drug anybody takes was tried first in animals."

By the same token, today's animal research may lead to better medicine in the future. Right now, researchers at the University of California School of Medicine, Davis, are infecting Asian rhesus monkeys with the simian AIDS virus, to see whether early treatment with the drug AZT will keep them from developing symptoms. Because the monkeys normally get sick within 10 months of infection— not the three to five years common in humans—the study will determine quickly whether the same treatment might save human lives.

At Houston's Baylor College of Medicine, Glen Martin and Brenda Lonsbury-Martin are using rabbits to study the hearing loss caused by environmental noise. By attaching small speakers to a rabbit's ears, the researchers can give the animal a large daily dose of noise resembling that of a blow-dryer or a factory or a construction site, and plot its effect. Knowing exactly how particular kinds of noise affect hearing would, of course, help us avoid the most dangerous ones. It might also suggest strategies for cleaning up the auditory environment.

At Emory University's Yerkes Center, other researchers are performing cataract surgery on healthy baby rhesus monkeys, hoping to devise better postsurgical therapies for the human children who undergo the operation. After performing the surgery, neurobiologist Ronald Boothe and his colleagues give different monkeys slightly different rehabilitative treatments, all of which involve placing an opaque contact lens over the good eye and a corrective lens in the wounded eye. After a year of therapy, the researchers kill the animals and dissect their brains to see which treatment has promoted the most development within the visual cortex. "We have kids being born who are going to go blind without this research," Boothe says. "By me doing this research, we can prevent them from going blind. Most people, given that choice, will think it's justified."

Ethical Concerns

If the issue were that simple, animal experimentation might never have become so controversial. But as the philosopher Peter Singer demonstrated in 1975, it's not. In a book called "Animal Liberation," Singer questioned the assumption that securing practical benefits for mankind automatically justifies experimentation on the other animals. Indeed, he condemned that notion as "a form of prejudice no less objectionable than prejudice about a person's race or sex," and he urged that we "consider our attitudes from the point of view of those who suffer by them."

To provide that perspective Singer had only to recount what scientists themselves had written in mainstream professional journals. In a chapter titled "Tools for Research," he sampled the recent literature from such diverse fields as toxicology and psychology, and it wasn't easy reading. He described standard government tests in which beagles were fed pesticides or bombarded with radiation until they lay bleeding from the mouth and anus. And he recounted numerous experiments in which psychologists subjected intelligent animals to fear or hopelessness or "psychological death" in crude attempts to analyze these emotional states.

In a 1972 paper in the Journal of Comparative and Physiological Psychology, for example, researchers at the Primate Research Center in Madison, Wis., described placing baby monkeys alone in a stainless-steel tank for periods of up to 45 days. They wanted to see whether confinement in this "well of despair" would cause lasting psychological damage. It did. The animals exhibited what the researchers termed "severe and persistent psychopathological behavior of a depressive nature." But the paper stressed the preliminary nature of this finding, saying further studies were needed to determine whether the symptoms could be "traced specifically to variables such as chamber shape, chamber size, duration of confinement [or] age at time of confinement." (No such experiments have been conducted at the Madison center since 1974.)

In other papers, the same scientists described efforts to gauge the effects of child abuse on young monkeys. In one experiment they designed mechanical surrogate mothers who would eject sharp brass spikes as the youngsters hugged them. The experience seemed to have no serious effect; the infants "simply waited until the spikes receded and then returned and clung to the mother." So, in a refinement of the experiment, the researchers forcibly impregnated females who had been driven mad through social isolation, and turned them loose on their own offspring. "One of [the mothers'] favorite tricks," they wrote, "was to crush the infant's skull with their teeth."

These programs were not mere atrocities, Singer argued. They were examples of scientists "doing what they were trained to do, and what thousands of their colleagues do." The peer-reviewed journals were brimming with similar stories. Researchers studying how punishment affects learning suspended dogs in hammocks and administered shocks through electrodes taped to their paws. Other investigators, curious to know how various drugs would affect a subject's responsiveness to punishment, implanted electrodes near pigeon's genitals, gave them drugs, then shocked them every time they pecked keys they'd learned to associate with food.

The Role of Activism

If Singer's work gave birth to a new social movement, a young activist named Alex Pacheco helped it grow. Pacheco, who was moved by Singer's book to help organize the group People for the Ethical Treatment of Animals (PETA), took a job in 1981 as a lab assistant at the Institute for Behavior Research in Silver Spring, Md. Once he had his own keys, he was able to spend several months sneaking in at night to document the mistreatment of 17 monkeys being used in a study of spinal-cord injury. Researchers had severed nerves to the monkeys' arms and were testing their ability to use the crippled limbs by shocking the animals when they failed. Pacheco's widely publicized photographs showed monkeys covered with open, infected wounds. Some had chewed the ends off their fingers. All were confined to filth-encrusted cages just a foot and a half wide.

Since then, similarly troubling conditions have come to light at a number of respected research centers. Yet all parties seem to agree that the general situation has improved markedly since 1980. The number of animals destroyed in experiments, however staggering, has declined steadily as researchers have come up with cheaper and more humane alternatives, such as cell cultures and computer models. And scientists using live animals have, as a general rule, become more conscientious and more accountable. "A lot of people are learning, a lot trying," says Ingrid Newkirk, the

British-born activist who founded PETA with Alex Pacheco eight years ago.

One of the first tangible changes came about in 1985, when Congress passed a series of amendments to the federal Animal Welfare Act, the law governing animal care in laboratories and other nonfarm facilities. The amendments have yet to be implemented by the Department of Agriculture, which enforces the act (they remain stalled in the federal budget office). But they mark a new congressional commitment to the "three R's" preached by moderate groups like the Animal Welfare Institute and the Humane Society of the United States: *reduction* in the number of animals sacrificed, *refinement* of techniques that cause suffering and *replacement* of live animals with simulations or cell cultures.

Specifically, the amendments call for the creation of a national data bank that will list the results of all animal experiments and thus prevent needless repetition. All laboratories using live animals are required, under the amendments, to set up animal-care committees and submit to annual inspections. Facilities housing dogs must let them exercise, and those housing primates must provide for their "psychological well-being."

Conditions Improving

Rather than wait for the new rules to go into effect, many institutions have adopted reforms on their own. Most research facilities—including all that receive funds from the National Institutes of Health—now have committees that review proposed animal experiments. And some primate facilities, such as Yerkes and New York University's LEMSIP (Laboratory for Experimental Medicine and Surgery in Primates), are going out of their way to keep the animals mentally and emotionally stimulated. To encourage social contact among the 250 chimpanzees that LEMSIP uses in AIDS and hepatitis research, veterinarian James Mahoney has constructed wiremesh tunnels between their cages. If an experiment requires keeping the animals separated, he makes sure they can see each other through sheets of Plexiglass. And to ward off the boredom that can turn lab chimps into blankeyed psychotics, he gives them games.

He may place tubs of frozen Kool-Aid outside the chimps' cages, then give them pieces of plastic tubing that can be used as long-distance drinking straws. Noodling tube into tub for an occasional sip can provide hours of entertainment. In a variation on the theme, Mahoney passes out plastic tubes stuffed with raisins and marshmallows and lets the chimps use willow branches to extract the treats, just as they would termites from a hollow log in the wild. The animals' latest craze is cleaning their own teeth with toothbrushes and admiring the results in hand-held mirrors.

The reforms haven't been confined to research laboratories. For 50 years, consumer-protection laws have effectively required that cosmetics and household products be tested on animals before being sold to humans. But major firms have recently started seeking, and finding, less noxious methods of quality control. The LD-50 test, which consists of gauging the dose of a given substance needed to exterminate half of the animals in a test group, is already falling by the wayside; a survey by the Food and Drug Administration shows that its use has declined by 96 percent since the late 1970s. The Draize test for irritancy, which involves squirting high concentrations of possible irritants into the eyes of rabbits, is still the industry standard. But Procter & Gamble now exposes rabbits to concentrations somewhat closer to those a consumer might encounter. And it has joined other firms in pledging to halt all animal tests as soon as alternatives are available.

Still, the changes of the past decade hardly signal a new consensus on the proper use of animals. Some scientists consider the reforms excessive. University of Mississippi physiologist Arthur Guyton, for example, warns that the trend toward stricter regulation threatens the very future of science. Even the 1985 amendments to the Animal Welfare Act could prove ruinously expensive, he says. The "very arbitrary" rules governing cage size might force labs all over the country to renovate their facilities. "While medical research using animals has not been killed outright," Guyton concludes, "it is slowly bleeding to death."

Activists, for their part, complain that the reforms have been too modest. A lot of needless suffering is still being perpetrated in the name of science and medicine, they say. Consider the situation at Sema Inc., a government contract laboratory in Rockville, Md., where AIDS and hepatitis experiments are conducted on chimpanzees. Visitors aren't normally welcome, but the renowned primatologist Jane Goodall got a tour of the facility last year, and later wrote an article for *The New York Times,* describing what she saw.

Unlike LEMSIP's chimps, Sema's spend years of their lives in total isolation, confined to tiny boxes that resemble nothing so much as microwave ovens. After watching a chimp stare blankly into space as her caretaker approached, Goodall wrote, "I shall be haunted forever by her eyes and by the eyes of the other infant chimpanzees I saw that day. Have you ever looked into the eyes of a person who, stressed beyond endurance, has given up, succumbed utterly to the crippling helplessness of despair?" Katherine Bick, deputy director of the National Institutes of Health, denies that the situation is really so grim. She adds, as she did last spring, that larger, better cages are on the way. Meanwhile, says PETA's Pacheco, conditions sanctioned by the federal government are "needlessly driving intelligent animals insane."

Emptying the Cages

Even more divisive is the question of where science should be headed. Many activists dream of a day when all the cages are empty. "Our bottom line," says Newkirk, "is a day when there are no animals in labs." Researchers find that idea ludicrous. They tend to dismiss it as a product of ignorance ("People with no science education don't recognize that the pyramid of knowledge, built upon basic research, depends on animals," says one federal official), or of sentimentality ("a bizarre elevation of a touchy-feely, do-gooder's view of the world," in the words of Yerkes administrator Frederick King).

The moral dilemma behind all this bitterness was nicely crystallized in a recent report by the National Research Council. "Research with animals has saved human lives, lessened human suffering and advanced scientific understanding," the authors observe, "yet that same research can cause pain and distress for the animals involved and usually results in their death."

It would be nice, of course, if there were alternatives to vivisection that could deliver the same benefits without the death and suffering. But there is a limit to what can be accomplished with cell cultures and computer models. "You can't mathematically model this disease," says Murray Gardner, head of the U.C. Davis team studying early drug treatment in AIDS-infected monkeys. "You've got to experiment in a living system, where all the things we don't know about are going on."

The question is whether the practical benefits of vivisection constitute a moral justification for it. If mankind's interest in finding a better treatment for AIDS *doesn't* justify conducting lethal experiments on individual humans, an ethicist might ask, why does it justify performing them on monkeys? Why doesn't a monkey deserve moral consideration? What is the relevant difference between a human subject and an animal subject?

To reply that the human is *human* and the animal isn't only begs the question. Peter Singer likens it to sanctioning racial discrimination on the ground that white people are white and black people aren't. Another possible answer is that we humans enjoy certain *God-given* prerogatives. We are, after all, the only creatures the Bible says were made in God's image. "Most Judeo-Christian religions make distinctions about the special nature of man," says Frederick Goodwin, director of the Alcohol, Drug Abuse and Mental

Health Administration. "To me, that is a distinct, qualitative difference between our primate relatives and man."

It may be a difference, but it's not an empirical, observable one. It has to be taken on faith. Are there certain things *about* humans that make us inherently more valuable than other animals? Language and rational thought are the two traits usually cited as setting *Homo sapiens* apart. Yet there are plenty of humans who *lack* language and reason—babies, the senile, the insane—and the thought of performing medical experiments on them is abhorrent. Why, if a severely retarded child is too precious to sacrifice, is a chimp of superior intelligence fair game?

Maybe there is no reasoned moral justification. Maybe animal experimentation is best understood in purely practical terms, not as a prerogative or an obligation but as a strategy for survival. Whatever the answer, scientists can no longer afford to pretend that their critics' moral concerns are frivolous. Profound questions are being raised, and ignoring them won't make them go away.

An Animal Rights Platform

ANIMAL RIGHTS NETWORK

The following document was originally published in the No-
vember 1987 issue of Animals' Agenda *by the Animal Rights*
Network, an animal rights advocacy group that ran the mag-
azine. It lists twelve important goals for the animal rights
movement. Although not everyone who supports animal
rights or animal welfare would agree that all twelve goals
are important, the list shows that by the late 1980s, the issues
involved in animal rights had broadened well beyond ani-
mal experimentation. The Animal Rights Network was
founded in 1979 and is today known as the Institute for Ani-
mals and Society.

1. We are firmly committed to the eventual abolition by law of animal research, and call for an immediate pro-hibition of painful experiments and tests.

The billions of dollars disbursed annually by the Na-tional Institutes of Health for animal experiments should be rechanneled into direct health care, preventive medi-cine, and biomedical research using non-animal tests and procedures. In addition, the government should fund pro-jects to develop and promote non-animal technologies where they do not yet exist so that animal experiments may be rapidly phased out. In the meantime, procedural mechanisms must be established to allow for greater pub-lic scrutiny of all research using animals.

2. The use of animals for cosmetics and household product testing, tobacco and alcohol testing, psychological testing, classroom demonstrations and dissection, and in weapons development or other warfare programs must be outlawed immediately.

3. We encourage vegetarianism for ethical, ecological, and health reasons.

As conversion of plant protein to animal flesh for human consumption is an energetically inefficient means of food production, a vegetarian diet allows for wiser use of the world's limited food resources. Livestock production is a major source of environmental degradation. Furthermore, a shift in human diet from animal foods to plant food would result in a lower incidence of heart diseases and cancer and better health generally. Vegetarian meals should be made available to all public institutions including primary and secondary schools. Nutritional education programs currently administered by the Department of Agriculture should be handled by an agency charged with promoting public health rather than promoting the interest of agribusiness.

4. Steps should be taken to begin phasing out intensive confinement systems of livestock production, also called factory farming, which causes severe physical and psychological suffering for the animals kept in overcrowded and unnatural conditions.

As animal agriculture depletes and pollutes water and soil resources, and destroys forests and other ecosystems, we call for the eventual elimination of animal agriculture. In the meantime, the exportation of live farm animals for overseas slaughter must be regulated to ensure humane treatment. Livestock grazing on US public lands should be immediately prohibited. Internationally, the US should assist poorer countries in the development of locally-based, self-reliant agricultural systems.

5. The use of herbicides, pesticides, and other toxic agricultural chemicals should be phased out.

Predator control on public lands should be immediately

outlawed and steps should be taken to introduce native predators to areas from which they have been eradicated in order to restore the balance of nature.

6. Responsibility for enforcement of animal welfare legislation must be transferred from the Department of Agriculture to an agency created for the purpose of protecting animals and the environment.

7. Commercial trapping and fur ranching should be eliminated.

We call for an end to the use of furs while recognizing Western society's responsibility to support alternative livelihood for native peoples who now rely on trapping because of the colonial European and North American fur industries.

8. Hunting, trapping, and fishing for sport should be prohibited.

State and federal agencies should focus on preserving and re-establishing habitat for wild animals instead of practicing game species management for maximum sustainable yield. Where possible, native species, including predators, should be reintroduced to areas from which they have been eradicated. Protection of native animals and plants in their natural surroundings must be given priority over economic development plans. Further, drainage of wetlands and development of shore areas must be stopped immediately.

9. Internationally, steps should be taken by the US government to prevent further destruction of rain forests.

Additionally, we call on the US government to act aggressively to end international trade in wildlife and goods produced from exotic and/or endangered fauna or flora.

10. We strongly discourage any further breeding of companion animals, including pedigreed or purebred dogs and cats.

Spay and neuter clinics should be subsidized by state and municipal governments. Commerce in domestic and exotic animals for the pet trade should be abolished.

11. We call for an end to the use of animals in entertainment and sports such as dog racing, dog and cock fighting,

fox hunting, hare coursing, rodeos, circuses, and other spectacles and a critical reappraisal of the use of animals in quasi-educational institutions such as zoos and aquariums.

These institutions, guided not by humane concerns but by market imperatives, often cruelly treat animals and act as agents of destruction for wild animals. In general, we believe that animals should be left in their appropriate environments in the wild, not showcased for entertainment purposes. Any animals held captive must have their psychological, behavioral, and social needs satisfied.

12. Advances in biotechnology are posing a threat to the integrity of species, which may ultimately reduce all living beings to the level of patentable commodities.

Genetic manipulation of species to produce transgenic animals must be prohibited.

Extreme Tactics Have Saved Countless Animals

NO COMPROMISE

The following piece was published anonymously in No Compromise, *a magazine that calls itself "the militant, direct action publication of grassroots animal liberationists and their supporters." It offers a sympathetic look at the Animal Liberation Front's lab raids of the 1980s. The lab raids typically involved a small group of activists breaking into a lab, freeing research animals, destroying equipment, and making off with records, photographs, and videotape that documented apparent animal suffering. The lab raids, while controversial because of the illegal tactics involved, were influential in pushing debate over animal rights into the public eye. As the author notes, on several occasions the public airing of videotape seized in the raids shocked ordinary Americans and led to substantial changes in laboratory research protocol. By the 1990s, for instance, most research labs across the country had tightened security.*

The 1984 raid of the University of Pennsylvania marks the A.L.F.'s [Animal Liberation Front's] greatest lab raid success.

On May 28 the Animal Liberation Front picked the lock to Thomas Gennarelli's head injury research lab at the University of Pennsylvania, smashing every piece of equipment in the lab and confiscating over 60 hours of Gennarelli's own research footage on his head smashing experiments with live primates. Gennarelli, who had for years hidden behind a laboratory door and thumbed his nose at animal advocates, had just met the animal rights movement's new answer to vivisection secrecy: the A.L.F.

The footage revealed the most horrific glimpse inside a vivisection lab ever seen before or since: 60 hours of inadequately anesthetized primates plastered into restraining devices receiving blows to the head at up to 1000 times the force of gravity. The video brought the evil of animal research to the attention of the nation and its "reallocation" became the A.L.F.'s most publicized action ever.

The A.L.F. of the 1980s found its greatest voice in PETA [People for the Ethical Treatment of Animals], who acted as a mouthpiece for the A.L.F. following the raids, holding press conferences and distributing videos and seized documents to the media. The PETA press conference following the Gennarelli raid set off a media-wildfire surrounding the confiscated footage and sparked a fierce standoff between the compassionate public and the animal researchers. The biomedical research PR machine swung into motion, reassuring an outraged public of the "necessity" of head injury research. They said the choice was simple: the baboons or their children.

The A.L.F. responded two months later by breaking into the University of Pennsylvania Vet School and liberating one dog.

A witchhunt was already underway for the A.L.F. raiders, introducing to the movement the now routine grand jury. High-profile animal rights activists and PETA employees were subpoenaed to answer questions before a panel closed to the public. The A.L.F.'s answer to these attempts at neutralization and to the blatant lies of vivisectors came 4 days after the previous break-in: U of P Vet school raided—four cats, one dog and eight pigeons were liberated. The A.L.F. strikes again.

When the smoke cleared it was a victory for the A.L.F. and the animals: NIH [National Institutes of Health] funding was revoked and Gennarelli's lab was shut down.

From one lab to the next throughout the '80s, the Animal Liberation Front saw the suffering, the torture, the legal means ignored, and implemented their timely and direct reaction to the slaughter—break down the doors, smash the labs, get the animals out. The U of P break-ins displayed what best characterized the A.L.F. raids of the '80s—a sense of urgency. And the A.L.F. never rested long.

Targeting Universities

By the end of 1984, the East Coast had seen 10 lab break-ins compared to the West Coast's three. In the east were NYU Medical Center (1 cat, 2 dogs, 2 guinea pigs), University of Southern Florida (55 gerbils, 35 rats), University of Massachusetts (2 rabbits), University of Maryland (42 rabbits), Howard University (30 cats), US Naval Medical Research Institute (1 dog), US Naval Medical Research Institute (3 dogs), Johns Hopkins University (6 rats), University of Pennsylvania and University of Florida (many rats), and in the west were UC Berkeley (3 cats), UCLA Harbor Medical Center (12 dogs), and Cal State Sacramento (23 rats). December 1984 would put the West Coast A.L.F. on the map and mark the first in a wave of high profile, expertly planned and executed lab break-ins in California during the mid '80s.

Tips from an inside whistleblower filtered down to A.L.F. operatives during 1984 and led to the highly publicized raid on the City of Hope cancer research labs in Duarte, suburban LA.

The A.L.F.'s source inside the lab allowed the band pre-raid entry into the facility, where the A.L.F. noted numbers and varieties of animals, allowing time to arrange homes for the freed prisoners from what would be the A.L.F.'s largest lab liberation to date.

During the early morning hours of December 9, 1984, the Animal Liberation Front gained access to the City of Hope labs via a door left open by the inside hand, destroyed over a half-million dollars in research, and loaded up 13 cats, 18 rabbits, 21 dogs, 50 mice and dozens more. The A.L.F.—115; City of Hope—zero.

The City of Hope raid showcased the 1980s' expertly orchestrated media campaigns where the highest importance was placed on projecting a Robin Hood–image to the public, and releasing confiscated research documents and video to the media to expose the fraud and lies of animal research. Through post-raid media coverage, the A.L.F. brought vivisection to the forefront and expedited its demise swifter than the hundred years of legal protest that preceded them.

A crucial realization led to this approach—the animals that they liberate always seem to get replaced. The A.L.F. never lost sight of the importance of individual lives, but it was the ripple effect of the A.L.F. raids during the '80s that proved to save the most animals in the long term. Job #1: Liberate. Job #2: Expose. It was the A.L.F.'s steps to "expose" which would ultimately be the vivisectors' biggest threat and what would bring the A.L.F. and the animals their greatest victories.

Video documentation and seized research logs from the raid had the most damaging effect on the City of Hope. When it was all over, City of Hope lost $700,000 in research, many experiments were permanently ended and, citing Animal Welfare Act infractions, the NIH suspended $1 million in funding. Another victory, but the A.L.F. was only getting started.

A Sophisticated Operation

By 1985, the West Coast had an active, expertly skilled A.L.F. cell coupled with safehouses and a highly efficient underground railroad. A.L.F. cell members were closely linked with known aboveground animal rights groups. Underground activists had positions inside such groups, intercepting whistleblower tips about research facilities and utilizing the help of sympathetic volunteers at mainstream groups who passed down information gained from such calls. The West Coast cell was quick to utilize the information from concerned employees, research assistants, students and vet techs passed to them, often warming up to and nurturing whistleblowers for their assistance in gaining access to the labs. It was through one such inside hand that the A.L.F. pulled off what would be it's most ambitious raid yet, and left authorities wondering, "How did they get in?"

During the early morning hours of April 20, 1985, the Animal Liberation Front gained access to the psychology labs at the University of California at Riverside, removed laboratory doors from their hinges, and liberated nearly 1000 animals. When vivisectors arrived the next morning, they found their labs trashed. Property damage exceeded $700,000. "Research," vice chancellor of the university said, "has been set back years."

It was the A.L.F.'s largest liberation ever—21 cats, 9 opossums, 38 pigeons, 70 gerbils, 300 mice, 300 rats, 300 rabbits, and a little baby monkey named Britches.

Britches was an infant macaque, the subject of a sight deprivation experiment since birth. When the A.L.F. released video footage of Britches—only slightly larger than a human hand, an electronic implant taped to his tiny head, eyes sewn shut—it was a PR disaster for the biomedical research industry. News coverage of the UC Riverside raid and Britches, the baby monkey, elicited an emotional and outraged response from much of the public, forcing the vivisectors to answer for the unjustifiable cruelty revealed by the raid—starved pigeons, mutilated opossums, cats with eyes sewn shut, and a showpiece in the war against vivisection—a little baby monkey named Britches. News coverage and public response to the A.L.F. rescue missions of the '80s contrast sharply to "terrorist" portrayal in media reports of the contemporary A.L.F. The public and media, it seemed, were in love with the A.L.F.

That the A.L.F. affected permanent change was undeniable. Eight of the 17 experiments interrupted by the A.L.F. at UC Riverside were never begun again. The psychology department no longer allowed baby monkeys' eyes to be sewn shut. Heat was installed to the outdoor primate colony. And one vivisector quit animal research forever.

During the early morning hours of October 26, 1986, the Animal Liberation Front entered the Science I building at the University of Oregon in Eugene, broke into 3 labs and rescued 264 animals from certain torture and death. Damage exceeded $120,000. There was no sign of forced entry.

The A.L.F. released a statement following the rescue stating, "This is just the beginning of our efforts to liberate those oppressed in research concentration camps in Oregon. We will not allow the slaughter to continue without resistance. You will hear from us again soon."

The raid brought into the spotlight the until-then-unknown bloody career of Barbara Gordon-Lickey a researcher at the University, who for over 17 years had tortured over a hundred kittens in pain research experiments and was the stated target of the break-in: "This freedom raid, which included the destruction of instruments inside these torture chambers, was directed at a butcher known as Barbara Gordon-Lickey, and in retaliation for the hundreds of innocent kittens she has murdered in the name of science."

The communiqué went on to explain the finer tactical points of research equipment destruction: "(a) $10,000 microscope was destroyed in about 12 seconds with a 36-inch steel wrecking bar that we purchased at a Fred-Meyer store for less than five dollars. We consider that a pretty good return on our investment." The statement continues, "the primate stereotaxic device . . . (is) one of the most sinister instruments of torture ever devised by the human mind. We took particular delight in destroying it."

The University of Oregon raid showcased what has been proven in break-in after break-in to ultimately be the A.L.F.'s most damaging tactic—the confiscation of damning documents and photos. The U of O raiders seized veterinary logs, cage notes, and over 400 photographs—many of the most graphic ever obtained by the animal rights movement. The photographs revealed the callousness of the vivisectors and the barbarity of their "research." One photo-series contains a gruesome "staged caesarian delivery," showing a clearly terrified baby monkey being "delivered" from the stomach of a female researcher. These photos, taken by researchers of each other as they abused and made fun of animals, were released to the media at press conferences in Eugene and LA following the raid.

The confiscated photos proved, once again, to be a PR disaster for the researchers. The University quickly moved the "evidence" of such violations as seen in the photos—the remaining primates—to a secret location elsewhere on campus.

Once again the A.L.F. exposed, in a high profile raid, absolute proof of blatant animal abuse inside vivisection labs. And once again the researchers repeated form-response after form-response that the raided facilities were "isolated instances," "an embarrassment to all research" and "not the norm." To alert members of the public, this was becoming difficult to accept.

The University of Oregon brought the movement its second A.L.F.-related arrest.

The night of the University of Oregon rescue Roger Troen, a known animal advocate, received an anonymous phone call. The caller asked Roger if he could drive to Eugene without mentioning it to anyone and take some animals in desperate need of a home. No details were offered as to the animals' origin, though as Roger put it, "I didn't need to ask."

Weeks later a veterinarian who had been asked to examine the animals led the police to Roger. The court case that followed put the University of Oregon and its vivisectors on the witness stand where the "scientists" were forced to describe their careers and the barbaric research protocols taking place inside their labs, bringing the vivisectors out from behind the walls of secrecy where they would prefer to hide.

Roger Troen received 6 months home detention and ordered to pay restitution for his role in the A.L.F.'s Underground Railroad. 10 rabbits were recovered and returned to the University labs. 254 animals were never located by investigators. Each one is an A.L.F. victory.

Firebombing and Arson

The next lab attack brought to America the A.L.F.'s most effective tool against animal abuser Naziism, introducing a strategy of "maximum destruction, not minimum damage," and setting the direction of large-scale A.L.F. actions for much of the next 15 years.

On April 16, 1987, the under-construction Animal Diagnostic Lab at UC Davis was firebombed. The animal research lab designed to cater to the needs of the food-animal industry burned to the ground. Damage was at $4.5 million. It is the most expensive A.L.F. action to date.

It was on that night the American A.L.F. gave birth to its most functional tool to directly render the instruments and structures of animal torture permanently inoperable. Circumventing the effort, risk, and limited damage of a nighttime live liberation after the lab's completion, the A.L.F. simply erased the Animal Diagnostics lab from existence.

After Davis, the fire bombings continued through northern California with further actions claimed by the Animal Rights Militia, including a $10,000 fire at the San Jose Veal Company warehouse, followed by a $230,000 fire at the Ferrara Meat Company. Two days later a poultry warehouse was set on fire and sustained $200,000 in damages. The A.L.F. took credit. The arson campaign continued into 1988 with the firebombing of the San Jose Meat Company, burning the building to the ground, and the torching of a fur store in Santa Rosa. The store never reopened. But the A.L.F., as they say, was only "warming up."

Using bolt cutters, crowbars, and blueprints retrieved

from laboratory dumpsters, A.L.F. freedom fighters systematically raided four buildings at the University of Arizona in Tucson on April 3, 1989, setting two fires, burning one building to the ground, doing nearly $300,000 in damages and liberating over 1,200 animals. It was the largest live laboratory liberation to date and arguably the most monumental A.L.F. action ever.

The raid began in the early morning hours when A.L.F. operatives broke into a ground floor door of the Bio-West building, took an elevator to the sixth floor, and wheeled out 965 animals before destroying the labs. Simultaneously across campus at the Shantz building, a second team removed an air vent cover approximately 12 feet off the ground, entered an airshaft and broke into a ground floor laboratory. Soon after, raiders broke into a ground floor door at the Microbiology/Pharmacy building, took an elevator to the sixth floor, and rescued additional animals.

Once the animals were out, one lab and one autopsy room was destroyed, the walls soaked in gasoline and the entire area torched. The team then moved off campus where an incendiary was placed under the building housing the office of the UA's director of animal research. The building and all contents were destroyed. Damages neared $300,000, and 1,231 animals were out of the vivisectors' lethal reach.

National news articles after the rescue called it a "Rambo-style remake of the story of Noah's ark."

A police report following the raid testified to the precision of the action. In the ensuing investigation, the UAPD [University of Arizona Police Department] "found little or no physical evidence left behind." The police found "the organization . . . prepares extensively for its strikes, leaves little or no evidence for police purposes, and operates at peak efficiency."

Investigators estimate the animal rescue and incendiary attacks took less than 90 minutes. "The A.L.F.," the report stated, "had thoroughly prepared for this attack." The police had no suspects.

A crucial and intended effect of A.L.F. actions, large or small, is the increase in the cost of killing animals. Following the rescue mission, campus police announced that as a direct result of the break-in, the University of Arizona had "to divest $1 million into animal research protection." By 5:00 PM the day of the raid, 24-hour security by off duty police was ordered at 11 campus research sites. This 24-hour security coverage continued for 6 weeks following the raid at a cost of $40,000 a week. Animal research labs scattered in 11 separate buildings throughout campus were consolidated into two secured facilities. The University of Arizona spent half a million dollars on new security following the raid to prevent against another A.L.F. break-in. With the University of Arizona raid, the A.L.F.'s statement was clear—the cost of torturing animals just went up.

A Quiet Decade

Direct action in the '80s ended with a break-in at John "Gorem" Orem's Texas Tech lab with 5 cats liberated and $70,000 damage to equipment. Less publicized raids took place into the early '90s with 6 rabbits liberated from a lab in Florida; 100 guinea pigs liberated from Simonsen Labs in Gilroy, CA; 750 mice, rats, and hamsters from a lab in Buffalo, NY; and 11 rabbits and 10 guinea pigs from Cook County Hospital in Chicago. These and the 4-state "Operation Bite Back" campaign to end the fur industry would be the A.L.F.'s final lab raids for several years.

Fast forward to 1999. Modern labs were perceived by many as being impenetrable. Lab liberations had been nonexistent for 7 years. Then, on April 5, 1999, ten years and two days after the University of Arizona raid, masked liberators broke into two separate buildings at the University of Minnesota rescuing 116 animals and using wrecking bars and sledgehammers to inflict a $2 million blow to vivisection.

It was the A.L.F.'s most triumphant comeback, setting off a wave of lab liberations and sabotage lasting through the end of the year. 1999 saw the liberation of 193 animals from medical research, more than the previous 9 years combined. Small-scale property damage of the early-mid '90s has given way to mink releases in great numbers, large scale arsons, and now, thanks to small cells of masked liberators with crowbars, the return of the lab raid.

The A.L.F. of the 1980s brought the horrors of vivisection from the shadows and formed the first true threat to the demons in their torture chambers who chose to murder the innocent. Month after month, throughout the 80s, many of these monsters found the Animal Liberation Front coming through their door.

To those demons who were not stopped and still continue—lock yourself inside because the storm is brewing again.

Illegal Tactics in Defense of Animals Are Sometimes Justified

PETER SINGER

In the 1980s there were numerous "direct action" campaigns against university laboratories and other research facilities that used animals in experiments. Typically, a small group of people would break into the labs at night to free the animals and destroy the research equipment. In the following article, Peter Singer argues that such unlawful, direct action in defense of animals is sometimes justified. According to Singer, citizens in a democracy are obliged to exhaust legal options before they turn to unlawful means. Nonetheless, he says, at certain times, the moral stakes are high enough that it is not immoral to break the law if doing so is the only way to achieve a morally worthy goal. Singer is a major figure in animal rights theory and a professor of philosophy at the Center for Human Values at Princeton University.

In 1939 Otto Schmidt was working as a laboratory assistant at a distinguished medical research institute in Germany. He learned, through chance remarks and his own observation, that another unit of the institute was receiving mentally retarded persons from a nearby asylum, and us-

Peter Singer, "To Do, or Not to Do?" *Hastings Center Report*, November/December 1989, pp. 42–44. Copyright © 1989 by The Hastings Center. Reproduced by permission of the publisher and the author.

ing them as research subjects. The patients were exposed to various poisonous gases, including nerve gas, and then forced to continue walking up and down an inclined ramp. They frequently vomited, and showed other symptoms of illness; but if they stopped, they were beaten with sticks. After a few days, most patients died from the poison gases they had inhaled; the remainder were put to death.

Schmidt was horrified by his discovery. At first he assumed that the scientists carrying out this research were doing so without authority, and that if the authorities were informed, it would be stopped. But his initial attempts to act on this assumption failed when the director of the institute made it clear that he had special permission from the highest levels to carry out this research "in the interests of the German soldier, who may again be exposed to chemical warfare." Schmidt attempted to contact these higher authorities, but he received no response. He also tried to alert the relatives of the patients, but his inquiries revealed that only patients who had no contact with relatives were selected for the experiments.

There was little more, legally, that Schmidt could do, but the experiments were continuing, and he could not simply forget about them. Therefore he decided on the only course of action he could think of that stood a chance of stopping the experiments. The unit conducting the experiments was housed in a separate, and specially equipped, building. One night, when neither staff nor experimental subjects were in the building, Otto obtained a supply of petrol and set fire to the building. His plan was entirely successful; the building was destroyed, and because of shortages of resources at the time, never rebuilt. No further experiments with poison gases were conducted at that research institute.

Judging the Defenders

What attitude should we take to what Otto Schmidt did? In criticism of his actions, it might be argued that he broke the law of his own country. Although he had certainly attempted to use legal channels to stop the research, it could not be said that he had exhausted all legal channels, since he had not received a definite and final response to his letters to higher authorities. It may also be said that Schmidt caused the destruction of a costly scientific research facility, and stopped a scientific research project that was adding to our knowledge about the capacities of human beings to continue working after exposure to harmful chemicals. Schmidt was not qualified, it might plausibly be asserted, to assess the scientific value of this work, nor its importance to the German Army.

Yet I do not think many of us will find these criticisms convincing. Schmidt was witnessing an atrocity. While the subjects of the experiments were suffering every day, he could not be expected to wait indefinitely for an official response—especially since this response might well be that the project should continue. As for the claim that Schmidt was not qualified to judge the value of the project, in this particular situation it seems clear that the project was unjustifiable. Schmidt did indeed use his own moral judgment on this matter, but his judgment was sound. For this—and also, of course, for his personal courage—he deserves not criticism, but the highest praise.

A Modern Comparison

Now consider a more recent incident:

At a prestigious research institute in the United States, monkeys were trained to run in a cylindrical treadmill. The monkeys received electric shocks unless they kept the treadmill moving. Once the monkeys had completed initial training at keeping the treadmill in motion, they were subjected to varying doses of radiation. Monkeys receiving the higher doses vomited repeatedly. They were then put back into the treadmill to measure the effect of the radiation on their ability to keep it moving. During this period, if a monkey did not move the treadmill for one minute, shock intensity was increased to 10 mA. (This is an intense electric shock, causing severe pain.) Some monkeys continued to vomit while in the treadmill. The irradiated monkeys took up to five days to die.

Animal liberationists learned that the institute was conducting these experiments. For several years they protested against them through a variety of legal channels, without success. Then an animal activist—let us call her Olivia Smith—succeeded in entering the laboratory in which these experiments were carried out and caused such damage to the laboratory and its equipment that the experiments stopped and were not resumed.

What attitude should we take to what Olivia Smith did? If we think that Schmidt was a hero, should we also think of Smith in the same way?

The criticisms noted in relation to Otto Schmidt's action will also be pressed against Olivia Smith. Do they have greater validity in her case than in his? Those who want to argue that Schmidt was a hero, but at the same time want to condemn Smith, will probably appeal first to the fact that the victims for whom Schmidt acted were human beings, whereas those saved by Smith's act were monkeys. I have elsewhere argued—and many other philosophers now agree—that species *in itself* cannot be a basis for this kind of distinction. It may be legitimate to treat differently beings with different capacities; but the mere fact that one being is a member of our species, and another being is not, cannot justify us in inflicting pain and death on the latter in circumstances that would not justify us in inflicting pain and death on the former.

So can we appeal to differences in the capacities of the beings involved in the experiments that took place in Germany and in the United States? We could only do this if our judgment about Schmidt's action was based on knowledge about the capacities of the subjects of the experiments he stopped. But we have no information on this matter—the subjects were described as mentally retarded, but how severely was not stated. Obviously, they were capable of walking, and of feeling pain. Equally obviously, so were the monkeys in the American experiment. There is no basis on which we can be confident that the human subjects were superior in respect of rationality, awareness, or any other possibly relevant capacity, to the nonhumans. In any case, if we were able to decide that Schmidt's actions were justified without inquiring more closely into the mental capacities of the human subjects, this strongly suggests that the existence of higher mental capacities—beyond the capacity to feel pain and to suffer from the poisonous gases— was not really relevant to our judgment. Accordingly, I conclude that our knowledge of any differences between the experimental subjects, whether in species or in capacities, is insufficient to serve as a basis for sharply differing judgments about what Schmidt and Smith did.

Unlawful Means as a Last Resort

The other factor likely to be put forward in explanation of why Schmidt was fully justified but Smith was not, is that Germany in 1939 was not a democracy, and there was no proper channel for stopping the experiments; in the United States, on the other hand, there are adequate opportunities for bringing about change through the democratic process. The differences between the political system are of immense significance. Although the United States is far from being a perfect democracy, we rightly treasure the opportunities it offers for peacefully and legitimately changing the laws of the country. In a society like the United States the obligation to try to bring about change by democratic means is very strong. If Olivia Smith's action had not been preceded by a long period of attempting to stop such experiments by lawful means, it would have been wrong. But such efforts *had* been made. They had been unavailing. The monkeys were continuing to go through extreme pain and suffering in the course of an experiment that was highly unlikely to bring significant benefits to humans or animals. In such circumstances, is the obligation to use only democratic means to bring about change an absolute one?

Though I am a strong supporter of democratic systems of government, even imperfect ones, I cannot believe that the obligation to use only democratic means is absolute. During the period of the civil rights marches, and later of protest against the Vietnam war, millions of Americans supported illegal forms of protest. Many of these involved breaches of racist segregation laws, and of the draft laws; some also caused damage to property, both private and government. It may be questioned whether such tactics were the most effective means possible to achieve civil rights for blacks, or to end the war in Vietnam; but this is a matter of strategy, not of ethics. If we can assume, for the sake of argument, that they were the *only* possible means of achieving those goals in a reasonable period of time, were they justified? I think they were. Even in a democracy, we can be justified in taking unlawful means to bring about change.

There is, I believe, a line to be drawn between acts that are illegal (including acts that cause specific and limited damage to property), and acts that inflict physical violence on others. A sound democracy can tolerate a certain amount of illegal protest; but violence against others is always likely to escalate quickly. More important still, when those who are acting on an ethical basis resort to violence, they obscure the clarity of their ethical stand and send a confused message to the public. Under a repressive dictatorship there may be no alternative to violence; but in a democracy, to resort to violence is to put in peril values that are greater than almost any cause.

Since Olivia Smith avoided inflicting physical violence on anyone, her act was not on the wrong side of this line. There may have been a much heavier burden of justification on Olivia Smith than on Otto Schmidt, but if her act, like his, was the only way to end an atrocity, she may also have been justified in what she did.

Justifying Direct Action

This is not a view I reach lightly. To encourage people to take the law into their own hands is a dangerous thing. There will be many people who regard as an atrocity acts that I do not see in the same light. Abortion is one obvious example. People who believe that a prenatal human being has the same right to life as an older human being are, in my view, misguided. In that respect I see a greater difference between Otto Schmidt and a pro-life activist who burns down an abortion clinic than I do between Otto Schmidt and Olivia Smith. Yet it is impossible to convince many pro-life people that they are mistaken, and so from their perspective, they too are entitled to the praise we bestow upon Otto Schmidt.

Reflecting on the position of those who do not share our views about what is right and what is wrong is salutary, because it makes us realize how great a responsibility we are under to think and think again about the judgment that what is happening is not merely wrong, but *so* wrong that it justifies taking the law into one's own hands. But where that judgment is clear; where it is a judgment that other reasonable people, fully informed of the facts of the situation, will share; where there is no other way of halting a continuing atrocity; where care is taken to avoid physical violence against anyone; then, and only then, do I believe direct action to be justifiable.

Otto Schmidt and Olivia Smith are imaginary, as are the German experiments I described. But I did not invent the experiments on monkeys. My account is drawn from a paper entitled "Effects of Mixed Neutrongamma Total-body Irradiation on Physical Activity Performance of Rhesus Monkeys," published in *Radiation Research* in 1985. The experiments took place at the Armed Forces Radiobiology Institute, in Bethesda, Maryland. As far as I am aware, similar experiments are still continuing.

The Use of Violence in Support of Animal Rights Is Wrong

JERRY SIMONELLI

In the following article, Jerry Simonelli argues that animal rights activists are morally obliged to refrain from resorting to violence in their pursuit of justice for animals. According to Simonelli, an attorney and former member of the Connecticut House of Representatives, animal rights activists should learn from the examples of Mohandas Gandhi, who led India to independence from British rule, and Martin Luther King Jr., an American civil rights leader. Although both Gandhi and King accepted that there were occasions upon which unjust laws deserved to be broken, neither thought violent action could be justified. Simonelli argues that resorting to violence and the destruction of property would be both wrong and counterproductive.

The animal rights movement is part of our wider struggle for peace, justice and respect for all beings and creation—what Albert Schweitzer referred to as a reverence for life. We lose our moral compass when we resort to the same hate and violence of those we seek to change. We must therefore resist the temptation to believe that force, violence or intimidation is justified—even if our motives are good.

Some in our movement claim adherence to the nonviolent philosophies of Mohandas Gandhi and Dr. Martin Luther King, Jr. yet participate in and/or condone acts of violence, intimidation and property damage. We must transcend mere lip service to the teachings of Gandhi and King and commit to their timeless and inspirational aspirations which inevitably lead to the uplifting of the human spirit. Neither Gandhi nor King advocated, condoned or participated in acts of violence, intimidation of persons, or destruction of property. Clearly, the civil disobedience strategies advocated by both—especially by King just before his death—were evolving. However, a careful study of the essences of their actions and words can lead only to their unwavering advocacy of strictly non-violent means. . . .

Violence Against People

Our movement is comprised of people with varied opinions regarding what is and what is not violence and if admittedly violence, whether it should be embraced as a legitimate strategy. Some groups (ex: Justice Department) openly embrace violent tactics like letter bombs, poisoned razor blades in envelopes and assassination of vivisectors. Other groups (ex: Animal Liberation Front (ALF) and Stop Huntingdon Animal Cruelty (SHAC)) embrace intimidation, harassment, physical attacks and property destruction.

At our movement conferences, we can hear representatives of the ALF and SHAC spew their rhetoric and unfortunately, often get enthusiastic applause. Conference sponsors and movement leaders seem meekly silent, espousing diversity in the movement, letting all voices be heard, that it takes many divergent strategies to advance a movement, etc. I am sure we cannot envision Gandhi or King diminishing their moral authority by an accommodation to the more destructive forces and tendencies among some in their movements.

All acts of physical violence must be condemned as both immoral and counter-productive. Violence only affords a temporary illusion of a solution when in fact, it always sows the seeds of hatred in both the person committing the violence and the target of the violence and it ensures the inevitability of revenge, retaliation and the never ending cycle of violence. Effective and lasting change requires difficult choices and deep searching for solutions not initially obvious. The belief that we can ever achieve peace and non-violence towards all animals through violence is illusory and short-sighted. Addressing the root causes of exploitation and evil are much more complex than simply forcing behavior upon someone or some company. We must persevere in developing effective messages and strategies that resonate with the public consciousness and help ignite a paradigm shift. Everything else is chasing the wind.

Destruction of Property

We venture down a treacherous path when property is destroyed. We can only imagine the result if every individual enforced his/her subjective opinion on what constituted "legitimate" property by destroying someone else's property that was not in conformity. We can see a strong parallel analogy in the anti-abortion movement. They believe a fetus is a human and that abortion is murder. To them, abortion clinics are an abomination much as we view slaughterhouses, factory farms and vivisection labs. Are we willing to embrace a philosophy that condones and encourages them to destroy abortion clinics? To them, they may be "liberating" or "rescuing" the life of a helpless and defenseless baby. However, to others, they are interfering with the legal rights of women and as long as the mandate of the wider society as codified in the law says that a woman has a right to an abortion, the exercise of that right must be protected while also allowing anti-abortion advocates their rights to speech, assembly, political organizing, etc., to potentially change the law. And, we can envision numerous other physical places/things that some consider evil, not legitimate like commercial sex establishments, sweatshops employing indentured servants, gambling casinos, etc. Should the zealous opponents of these activities/places be encouraged to destroy them?

Some pose the difficult question of whether destruction of property is justified in the example where someone destroyed railroad tracks leading to the concentration camps. I believe one answer lies in whether the channels and mechanisms for change are totalitarianism or democratic. We live in an open society with established, legitimate mechanisms for effecting change where we are free to organize, mobilize and engage in acts of civil disobedience, non-cooperation and other strategies of constructive confrontation to communicate our ideas. We may not like the fact that most people (at least for now) do not agree with us but destructively confrontational tactics will not change the outcome nor advance a more enlightened consciousness.

Illegal Break-Ins and Rescues

Once we go beyond physical violence and destruction of property, the spectrum of alternative tactics becomes more difficult to neatly categorize as right or wrong and effective or ineffective. If one breaks the law and does so openly, non-violently and with a willingness to accept responsibility and consequences, and lovingly with the intention of conversion and reconciliation, the principles laid down by Gandhi and King are probably met.

The decision to engage in break-ins and rescues should be strictly scrutinized for necessity and effectiveness. The action may be more likely to elicit wider public support and sympathy if it is done strictly to document atrocities whereby laboratories, slaughterhouses and factory farms are themselves breaking federal and/or state law or to dramatize the inadequacies of laws in protecting animals and to educate the public on the inadequacies and resulting suffering and when proof can only be obtained through trespass.

However, duplicative break-ins and rescues, although significant to the individual suffering animal, may divert attention, energy and resources from real solutions by addressing symptoms of exploitation and indifference to suffering. By analogy, if abolitionists freed slaves from a particular plantation, it certainly benefited the individual slaves liberated but would it have really affected the underlying institution of slavery which was more reliant on factors like economics, custom, racism, etc.? Also, since illegal activities can lead to prosecution and imprisonment, barring the high profile jailing of a Gandhi or King (which of itself has the potential of consciousness raising due to the publicity), is going to jail not a waste of funds and precious time that could be used in more effective pursuits to alleviate the plight of animals.

Human society constantly struggles with outbreaks of violence and brutality despite universal norms of human rights. We are faced with an even greater challenge since we are seeking consideration, compassion and justice not for members of our own group, but for other species. What we are asking people to do is a fundamental shift in the way they view the world and to alter lifetime customs and behavior. In their own struggles, neither Gandhi nor King had all the answers when each embarked on uncharted waters and experiments in social action and they were often quite anguished over appropriate techniques. However, with deep reflection and trial and error each devised a strategy that worked while remaining consistent with and faithful to their principles. As we embark on our journey, we must resist the temptation to violence and hold the lives, teachings and examples of Gandhi and King as a guiding beacon.

Animal Rights Terrorism

WESLEY J. SMITH

In the following article, Wesley J. Smith, a senior fellow at the Discovery Institute, argues that animal rights activism has close links to terrorism. Smith notes that the FBI considers the Environmental Liberation Front to be one of the largest terrorist organizations in the United States and that other respected antiterrorist watch groups, such as the Southern Poverty Law Center, have pointed out terrorist tactics in the movement. Smith also argues that more mainstream animal rights organizations, such as People for the Ethical Treatment of Animals, support animal rights terrorism with funding and publicity.

When many people think of "animal rights," they may picture trendy celebrities posing in nude photographs to combat the fur industry. Or perhaps, they will roll their eyes and smile when they hear that the People for the Ethical Treatment of Animals (PETA) reported the California Milk Advisory Board to the FCC [Federal Communications Commission] for false advertising because its television ads claim "California cheese comes from happy cows."

But the animal-rights/liberation (ARL) movement isn't funny anymore. Unable to get most of society to agree that animals are the moral equals of people or that farming pigs is akin to holding human slaves, some ARL activists have crossed to the dark side—animal-rights terrorism. Indeed, violence, vandalism, and personal threats from groups such as the Animal Liberation Front (ALF), the Environmental Liberation Front (ELF), and Stop Huntingdon Animal Cruelty (SHAC) have ratcheted up so radically against medical researchers, ranchers, and others in recent years, that animal-rights terrorism is now being scrutinized by one of the most respected antiterrorist organizations in the world, the Southern Poverty Law Center (SPLC).

You have to be especially dangerous and potentially violent to warrant attention from the SPLC. Cofounded by renowned civil-rights attorney Morris Dees, the group is best known for its successful legal struggle against hate groups such as the Ku Klux Klan and Aryan Nation. One of the center's most useful projects is the respected SCLC Intelligence Report (IR), a quarterly magazine that offers in-depth analysis of political extremism in the United States. The Fall 2002 IR exposes the depth of the threat of ARL terrorism—earning ALF, ELF, and SHAC a level of infamy usually reserved for American extremist groups such as the KKK, Aryan Nation, and the American Nazi party.

Terrorist Tactics

According to the IR expose, "From Push to Shove," ARL terrorists such as ALF and SHAC regularly employ "death threats, fire bombings, and violent assaults" against those they accuse of abusing animals. Some of the cruelest attacks have been mounted by SHAC against executives for Huntingdon Life Sciences, a British drug-testing facility that uses animals to test drugs for safety before they are tested on people. Indeed, the threats and violence became so extreme that Huntingdon fled Britain out of the fear that some of their own were going to be killed. They had good cause: The company's managing director was badly beaten by three masked assailants swinging baseball bats, while another executive was temporarily blinded with a caustic substance sprayed into his eyes.

Unfortunately for Huntingdon, the ARL terrorist network

is international and a mere move across the Atlantic Ocean did not protect it. Not only has the terrorism continued here, but U.S. companies with business ties to the company have also been targeted.

This tactic, which has the goal of driving Huntingdon out of business, has already produced fruit. In Britain, SHAC terrorists caused Barclay's Bank to withdraw financing from Huntingdon when their executives came under assault. Similarly, after it was subjected to terrible threats and intimidation, the Stephens Group of Arkansas withdrew a promised $33 million loan. Now, Marsh USA and its executives have been warned by SHAC to revoke the insurance of a Huntingdon facility. To the company's credit, as yet it has not allowed ARL Brownshirts to dictate its business decisions—even when SHAC published executives' home addresses, phone numbers, and Social Security numbers. Meanwhile, according to the Intelligence Report, a United States-based Huntingdon vice president has been so badly and repeatedly harassed that the man's "wife is reportedly on the brink of a nervous breakdown and divorce."

Mainstream Support

The deafening lack of condemnation by mainstream ARL organizations against these terrorist tactics speaks louder than their oft-stated claims to being a peaceful social movement. Indeed, the firewall that groups such as PETA have long maintained between themselves and ARL terrorists seems to be breaking down. PETA's tax-exempt status is being challenged because it admittedly paid $1,500 to ELF. (According to the FBI, ELF is one of the nation's largest terrorist groups.) According to the SPLC, PETA also provided funds to convicted animal- or environmental-rights terrorists, including contributing $20,000 to Rodney Coronado, convicted of setting fire to a research lab at Michigan State College, and $7,500 to Fran Trutt, convicted of attempting to murder a medical executive.

The Intelligence Report also reveals that known ELF and

ALF activists are routinely invited to speak at the yearly Washington, D.C., animal-rights conference sponsored by PETA and the Humane Society of the United States. Further, the IR quotes PETA's Bruce Friedrich as stating:

If we really believe that animals have the same right to be free from pain and suffering at our hands, then of course we're going to be blowing things up and smashing windows. . . . I think it's a great way to bring animal liberation, considering the level of suffering, the atrocities. I think it would be great if all of the fast-food outlets, slaughter-houses, these laboratories, and banks that fund them, exploded tomorrow.

PETA should be roundly condemned for permitting one of its own to advocate violence and for associating with violent groups such as ALF. In this regard, it is worth pointing out that ALF has gone so far down the terrorist path that it posted a how-to-commit-arson manual on its website. Called "Arson Around with Auntie ALF," the tract promotes the use of incendiaries to destroy animal "abusing" facilities because "pound for pound" they "can do more damage than explosives against many types of targets." There is a downside, however, which ARL terrorists are advised to consider when deciding how to best carry out their planned attacks. During the "time lag" between the setting of the fire and "the destruction of the target," Arson Around warns, the "fire may be discovered and controlled or put out." Thus, even though it may do less damage, the upside of explosives is that "once detonated, [the explosion] has done its work."

Unlike hierarchical terrorist organizations such as al Qaeda that keeps close control over operations, the ALF terrorist manual urges its minions to adopt an anarchist approach. They are to join together in small cells of two or three people and never tell anyone about their ALF affiliation. When they carry out their assaults, they are instructed to spray-paint animal-rights slogans signed by "ALF" all over the crime scenes before fleeing. In that way, it will be all but impossible for law enforcement to infiltrate the terrorist cells or solve the crimes. Best of all, ALF will get the credit for the terror attack but its known organizers will honestly be able to claim that they had no foreknowledge of the plan or who actually carried out the attack.

Where do we go from here? Downhill, apparently. The SPLC Intelligence Report worries that "further violence seems almost inevitable" as animal-rights terrorist leaders inspire "a new breed of activist." Sooner or later, someone is likely to be killed.

This isn't alarmist rhetoric. In the Netherlands, an animal-rights extremist allegedly assassinated a candidate for parliament, perhaps because he defended pig farming in a debate with animal-rights activists. An ELF representative recently suggested that it might be time to "take up the gun," while the Intelligence Report quotes Kevin Jonas of SHAC-USA as personalizing JFK's famous quote, "If you make peaceful revolution impossible, you make violent revolution inevitable."

THE
HISTORY
OF
ISSUES

CHAPTER 4

Animal Rights and Scientific Progress

Scientists Have Responded by Using Fewer Animals

ECONOMIST

The following article, originally published in the Economist *magazine in 1995, explores how science has responded to animal rights concerns by adjusting experiment protocol. This "Three Rs" approach, as it is known, focuses on reducing, refining, and replacing. Scientists have reduced their number of animals used, in part because they have a greater concern with avoiding using animals in experiments when it is unnecessary. Furthermore, the* Economist *reports, the experiments themselves have been refined so that in many cases they cause less distress to animals and produce more information per animal. Finally, according to the* Economist, *science has responded by developing alternatives to animal experimentation. In many cases, for instance, scientists are able to use computer models, or experiments on bacteria, to replace traditional tests involving mammals.*

At present [1995] Britain is in the middle of an enormous fuss over the cruelty of exporting calves in crates. An issue that raises similar moral questions, and which divides the antagonists just as bitterly, is vivisection. That debate has a longer history. More than a century and a half ago Francois Magendie, a visiting French physiologist, ruffled London's sensibilities by carrying out experiments on animals in public. There were cries of protest, comments in the press, questions in Parliament and dark hints of cruelty on the Continent. Then, as now, there was little meeting of minds.

The quarrel between those who would endow animals with "rights" and those who say that animals must be used if science is to move forward remains as heated as ever. Many of the familiar arguments will be aired again during a week of protest and discussion in the United States and Europe that starts on April 24th—which an alliance of animal-welfare groups is calling International Laboratory Animal Day.

Yet the gap between those who care most about the welfare of animals and those who care most about scientific advance may soon be narrowed: not through agreement on the underlying moral question, but because fewer experiments on animals are going to be needed. Scientists, businessmen and policy-makers have been developing alternatives to the use of live animals for biomedical research and toxicology testing. They have made impressive progress.

The Three Rs

Their approach can be summed up in three words: reduce, refine and replace. That is, use fewer animals in tests and experiments; make the tests that remain necessary both more informative and more humane; and develop procedures in which animals no longer have to be used at all.

Worldwide figures for the animals used each year in research and testing are a matter of guesswork, since few countries require researchers to keep any records. National statistics for the countries that do, patchy though they are, point to a substantial decline in animal use over the past decade. British research "employed" 2.8 million animals in 1993, 100,000 fewer than the preceding year and 20% fewer than in 1987. Holland and Canada have reported similar reductions in their use of mammals.

It is harder to be sure about what is happening in the United States because the commonest experimental animals, mice and rats, are not under federal protection and are therefore not counted. Researchers estimate that, as in Britain, such rodents are used in 85% of current experiments. Andrew Rowan, director of the Tufts Centre for Animals and Public Policy in Massachusetts, reckons that the total number of animals used in American research has dropped by a half—to no more than 30m a year—since 1968. To an animal-welfare extremist, 30m is still a holocaust. Nonetheless, the trend is clear. At the end of the 1970s a single pharmaceutical company such as Hoffman LaRoche was consuming 1m animals a year in production and testing. Now they and other big corporate users such as Procter & Gamble, a consumer-goods company, and Avon, a cosmetics firm, have typically reduced their requirements by 90%.

One reason for the change is that governments have insisted on it. Western Europe leads the way in legislation: since 1986 a European Union directive, enforced by national committees, has instructed researchers to choose non-animal methods if they are "scientifically satisfactory [and] reasonably and practically available." The European Commission will ban almost all cosmetics testing on animals from 1998 and aims by 2000 to cut the number of animals used in research to half its present level.

In America, years of permissive legislation have been slowly amended to encourage reduction, refinement and replacement. The National Institutes of Health recently produced a plan for reducing the use of animals in its research, although it has been reluctant to speak of "alternatives". Louis Sibal, director of the NIH Office of Laboratory Animal Research, says that many scientists prefer the term "adjuncts", emphasising the role of new techniques as complements to rather than substitutes for animal-based research.

Public qualms over the use of animals seem unlikely to go away. Even in Switzerland, that bastion of pharmaceutical research, a 1992 referendum came within 7% of curtailing animal experiments. And with mounting public concern has come a flow of money to fund the development of alternatives. Barbara Orlans of the Kennedy Institute of Ethics in Washington, DC, says there are now tens of millions of dollars of financial support from more than 60 sources worldwide, ranging from companies and governments to humane societies.

It is one thing to call for alternatives to animal testing, and to pour money into the search. Can science deliver?

Alternatives to Animals

With the advent of molecular biology in the 1970s came the rise of micro-organisms as experimental tools. It has become cheaper and faster to see whether a substance is toxic by testing it on fungi and bacteria than by testing it on living animals.

Photobacterium phosphoreum, a luminescent bacterium, is particularly effective at detecting chemical irritants. During its normal metabolism, this bug converts part of its cellular energy into light. Certain classes of chemicals can interfere with this process and dim the glow, providing a way to measure their toxicity. A test based on it, first developed by scientists at Microbics Corporation in Carlsbad, California, is now used by companies such as Boots, a British drug firm, in their battery of tests.

Microbics has also introduced a dark version of this bacterium which has its lights turned on by mutation-inducing substances. Preliminary studies suggest that this system may prove as useful as the venerable Ames test. And yet it took nearly ten years of assessment to convince America's Environmental Protection Agency that the Ames test was sensitive and specific enough to predict human toxicity. The Ames test uses salmonella bacteria which respond in clearly recognisable ways to changes in their DNA. When the bacteria are exposed to a chemical which is being tested their response reveals any tendency in the chemical to produce mutations. Even today, it is one of the few microbial toxicity tests that international regulators have approved.

This sort of delay prompts people like Michael Balls, head of the new European Centre for the Validation of Alternative Methods in Ispra, Italy, to claim that the present barrier to replacing animals is as much bureaucratic as it is scientific.

But microbes can play the part of mammals in only so many settings; theirs is really a supporting role to the new star of test-tube methods, which is cell culture. Science has recently made rapid advances in understanding what it takes to make cells grow. This means that almost any cell can be taken from the body of an animal or a human and kept alive for days or even years.

These increasingly sophisticated techniques are the mainstay of modern cell biology because they allow scientists to study basic cellular processes in settings that are more accessible and flexible than whole animals. They can also lead to substantial cuts in the numbers of animals used to produce biological substances. Some vaccine reagents, which once demanded fresh tissue from animals, can now be grown in cell culture. Three decades ago, for example, Holland used 3,500 monkeys a year to produce its polio vaccine; now only 20 are needed.

Monoclonal antibodies, guided missiles of the immune system that are widely used in medical diagnosis and treatment, have usually been harvested from special tumours implanted in the abdomens of mice. Now new technologies, such as the hollow-fibre bioreactor, are allowing these antibodies to be produced efficiently *in vitro* and not in the bellies of beasts. Britain recently reported a one-year drop of 30% in the number of animals used to generate monoclonal antibodies. The use of such alternatives is compulsory in Switzerland.

Cell-culture methods are also having an impact on the use of live animals in drug testing and safety evaluation, a legal requirement in almost all countries. Before 1985, the American National Cancer Institute used to try out potential anti-cancer drugs on cancerous mice; by switching to human tumour cells, they have reduced the number of animals in these tests from more than 4m to about 1m.

A large number of cell-culture systems are now being developed to test substances quickly and easily for a tendency to cause cancer or birth defects. Some of the most innovative ideas are emerging from laboratories at Xenometrix in Boulder, Colorado. There, scientists have created lines of human cells which contain different "stress" genes whose activation by toxic chemicals is easily detected. These tests can tell not only whether, but also how, a given chemical harms a particular type of cell.

There is, however, a limit to what can be learnt from studying isolated cells. Most advocates of alternatives to animal testing accept that test-tube methods cannot replicate the intricacy of mammalian organs.

Attempts to reconstruct complex tissues—such as the liver—in the test tube have made slow progress. But there have been successes with other complex organs. Human skin, with its complex three-dimensional structure, is a case in point. Skin is no single layer but a stratification of specialised cells, proteins and fats: more of a biological millefeuille than a pancake. Maria Ponec's group at the University of Leiden in Holland has created a living test-tube equivalent of the outer two layers. With this they can study the skin's function as a biological barrier.

One of the most commercially successful of these artificial constructs is Skin<2>, developed at Advanced Tissues Sciences in La Jolla, California. Researchers there use cells from the off-cuts of routine circumcisions to construct sheets of fully differentiated, three-layered human skin on nylon scaffolds. By observing microscopic changes in tissue structure and measuring the rate at which cells release inflammatory substances, researchers can see whether compounds irritate the skin, as well as studying wound healing and psoriasis.

Skin<2> has proved so effective at detecting corrosive

chemicals that the American and Canadian transport departments last year approved it as a substitute for the traditional test used to classify such substances: applying them to the backs of shaved rabbits and watching them burn through.

Cosmetics Testing

Such rabbits had it easy compared with those on which the notorious Draize test for eye irritation is performed. This test consists of squirting chemicals into the eyes of a number of rabbits and seeing how the tissue changes. The cosmetics industry has spent the past decade looking hard for alternatives. Some consist of refining the present technique so that fewer rabbits or less of the chemical can be used without compromising the tests' results. Others use cell cultures or the membranes of fertilised hens' eggs to measure a compound's potential irritance.

As yet, however, not one of more than 60 alternative techniques has been officially accepted as a substitute for the Draize test, although international validation studies (of a sort, ironically, that the Draize test itself never had to go through) are in full swing. One of the simplest alternatives—EYTEX from In Vitro International in Irvine, California—is also among the most reliable. Many of the substances which cause this clear mixture of plant proteins and sugars to go cloudy also turn out to be irritants in the Draize test, a correlation which bodes well for its prospects as a replacement.

A more recent innovation is a technological spinoff from cataract research at the University of Waterloo in Canada. Jacob Sivak and his colleagues have devised a laser-scanning system to detect alterations in the optical properties of cattle eyes fresh from abbatoirs.

The lenses are placed in a solution which mimics their natural fluids and keeps them alive. Then a laser light is shone through them. Toxic insults to a lens will distort it, altering the path of the light in a way that can be recorded with a video camera. This provides a reproducible and objective measure of how much damage can occur to this essential pan of the eye, which the Draize test overlooks. Lenses can last for weeks in culture, so this system can also be used to gauge how long and how well the tissue will recover when an irritant is removed, a significant advantage over many other proposed alternatives.

Some scientists see the future of in vitro alternatives in the glass of a computer screen as well as at the bottom of a test tube. This is particularly true in toxicology, where mathematical models and computer programs are now used to predict the biological activity of compounds.

Such systems depend on a simple premise, that it is the atomic organisation of a molecule that accounts for its toxic properties. "Expert systems" such as a piece of software known as DEREK, developed by Chris Earnshaw and Derek Sanderson at Schering Agrochemicals, can spot suspect bits of atomic structure by comparing a molecule drawn on a computer screen to a database of molecules whose characteristics are known. Any matches with features associated with toxicity are highlighted as hotspots, for special attention in subsequent tests.

Equations known impressively as quantitative structure activity relationships—QSARs—are also used to give a precise description of the relationship between a compound's characteristics and a given toxic effect. Scientists at Unilever's laboratories in Bedford, England, have taken information about known eye irritants and created a QSAR which relates their molecular size, electronic charge and other properties to their capacity to cause injury in the Draize test. With this analysis in hand, it becomes possible to predict whether a similar chemical is likely to be an irritant without recourse to a rabbit.

Computer Models

However, computer models . . . are only as useful as the quality of the data with which they have been built. And although the world is brimming with databases of structures and toxicities, their quality varies widely. Some, like that of the toxicology programme at America's National Cancer Institute, are pretty reliable, but others are duds. As a result, there are now calls for an international chemical reference databank to consolidate dependable information from industry and the public domain, making the most of results from earlier live animal experiments so that unnecessary repetition can be avoided.

Computer methods such as these give snapshots of a compound's potential toxicity. But newer simulation models aim to provide a dynamic picture of its interactions throughout the body. The impact of a drug, for example, does not depend only on how it docks with a receptor on a target cell. The ways in which it is taken up into the body, passed through the circulation, altered in the liver, and finally expelled also matter. Using data from older, whole-animal research and more recent test-tube techniques, these processes can be represented mathematically and integrated to create a PBBK, or physiologically-based bio-kinetic model.

At present, computerised PBBK models are unable to predict the effects of novel substances, but an ambitious multi-centre European scheme aims to develop them. As part of this programme, Bas Blaauboer at the University of Utrecht is putting his PBBK models through their paces with known neurotoxins to see whether they can represent their interactions in the body. Robert Combes, director of the Fund for the Replacement of Animals in Medical Experiments, a charity which runs Britain's leading animal-alternatives centre, is hopeful that the time will come when the merest gleam in a pharmacologist's eye can be designed, tested, modified and approved all on the basis of a combination of these computerised models and *in vitro* alternatives.

But it is not just high-tech wizardry that is needed to reduce the number of animal experiments. In many cases, a reduction depends on the willingness of regulators to accept the alternatives, and to comply with one another's rulings. Hence the current flurry of validation studies to prove that the new options are adequate substitutes for established whole-animal methods.

In basic research, the emphasis is slightly different. Dr. Orlans believes that the most immediate gains will be made in refinement, not replacement, of experiments, making them as humane and informative as possible using the minimum number of animals. Biomedical science will continue to ask questions that, for the moment at least, only live-animal experiments can answer. The information they yield, however, can lead to new non-animal methods. With their professional societies, electronic bulletin boards, peer-reviewed journals, and a second "world congress" next year [1996] advocates of the three Rs are growing in scientific respectability, as well as in numbers.

The Benefits of Animal Research Are Worth the Cost

CARL COHEN

In the following excerpt from a debate over animal rights, philosopher Carl Cohen argues that the benefits of animal research to both humans and animals outweigh the costs of animal research in terms of suffering to animals. Cohen begins with a review of how important research on animals has been to the development of medicine. He points out that most of the scientists to whom the Nobel Prize in medicine has been awarded have used animals in their research, and he lists many of the areas in which animal experimentation has deepened human understanding of biological processes. Cohen also notes that developments in veterinary medicine have depended on animal research. Cohen concludes by asking his readers to weigh the total good produced by animal research against the total harm involved. He is convinced the scales tip definitely in favor of animal research.

I conclude with a brief backward look. Animal research is promising for the future precisely because we know how very great its accomplishments have been in the past, the recent past, and the long history of medicine. Here again it is impossible to report all contributions because they have been so many and so varied. Even a list would be too long.

So I propose, in what follows, to exhibit the historical

impact of animal research by noting how central animal studies have been to those who were awarded the Nobel Prize for medicine during the century that has just ended. The overwhelming majority of these Nobel awards have been made to scientists whose research was done using animal subjects.

In 1901, the Nobel Prize was awarded (to Emil von Behring) for the development of the antiserum to diphtheria, dependent on experiments with guinea pigs. In 1996, the Nobel was awarded (to Peter Doherty and Rolf Zinkernagel) for explanations of the workings of the human immune system in combating viruses, dependent on experiments with mice. In the years between, chickens and frogs, rabbits and monkeys, horses and rats, pigs and dogs, fish and sheep, as well as other species have contributed to Nobel Prize–winning research. This research has ranged from the monumental discovery of insulin for the treatment of diabetes (Frederick Banting and John Macleod in 1923 using dogs, rabbits, and fish) to the development of the yellow fever vaccine (Max Theiler in 1951 using monkeys and mice). The antibiotic streptomycin was developed using guinea pigs, resulting in the Nobel Prize for 1952 to its discoverer, Selman Waksman. Organ transplantation, to which thousands of humans now owe their lives, would have been impossible without the experiments of Joseph Murray and E. Donall Thomas using dogs, for which they received the Nobel Prize in 1990. The understanding of cholesterol and the regulation of fatty acids in humans was made possible by studies with rats, resulting in the Nobel Prize to Konrad Bloch and Feodor Lynen in 1964. How cancers can be induced by tumors, and treated with hormones, resulted in the Nobel Prize being awarded to Charles Huggins and Francis Rous in 1966 for their experiments with rats, rabbits, and hens. The role of adrenal hormones in combating arthritis was uncovered in studies using cows, for which the Nobel Prize was awarded to Edward Kendall, Philip Hench, and Tadeus Reichstein in

1950. Surgical techniques that are now taken for granted, the grafting of blood vessels and techniques of suture, could not have been developed without animal subjects, in this case dogs, in studies that resulted in the Nobel Prize award to Alexis Carrel in 1912. The understanding of the genesis of typhus, a deadly disease for most of human history, came only with experiments on pigs, mice, and rats by Charles Nicolle, who received the Nobel Prize for that work in 1928. And the genesis of tuberculosis, long the leading killer of humans, came only with experiments on cows and sheep, resulting in the Nobel being awarded to Robert Koch in 1905.

Indispensable Research

Fundamental understanding of the workings of the human body has repeatedly advanced by way of investigations with animals: the understanding of the central nervous system (using horses and dogs); of immunity (using rabbits and guinea pigs); of the role of vitamins (using chickens); of the function of neurons (using dogs and cats); of the working of the inner ear (using guinea pigs); of the processes of vision (using chickens, rabbits and crabs); of the genetic code (using rats); of antibacterial drugs (using mice and rabbits); of the specific functions of nerve cells (using cats); of the chemical structure of antibodies (in guinea pigs and rabbits); of the processing of visual information by the brain (using cats and monkeys); of the functional organization of cells (using chickens and rats)—for every one of which the Nobel Prize in medicine has been awarded. Almost endlessly the central role that animals have played in the history of medicine can be recounted. This very quick review gives evidence enough that animal subjects have been absolutely indispensable in medical research.

Readers of this book [*The Animal Rights Debate*, Carl Cohen and Tom Regan, Rowman & Littlefield, 2001], including those who criticize animal research, owe their personal safety and well-being, and the well-being of their children, to the animal research that some would have us shut down. Vaccines, antibiotics, prosthetic devices, therapeutic drugs of every description, the basic science that will make possible advances not yet dreamed of, as well as the safety of products we consume every day, are owed to animal research.

This momentous role that animals play in medical investigation is not widely enough understood. Unfamiliar with the reliance of research on animal subjects, unaware of the full range of its consequences and unprepared to cope with the technical complexities of human disease, too many give their support too readily to organizations quite mistakenly suggesting that animal investigations can be replaced by computers or by human clinical studies. That supposition is utterly false. A committee consisting of fourteen of the most distinguished living physicians, the Council on Scientific Affairs of the American Medical Association, concluded categorically in 1989, "Research that involves animals is essential to improving the health and well-being of the American people."

Animals Helping Animals

Not only humans but animals as well have benefited enormously from animal studies. Every pet owner, as well as all those who work with horses, sheep, or cows or other species in animal husbandry, and also those concerned to protect and preserve animals in the wild, may be grateful for the research that has been done using animals to keep animals healthy and to extend their lives.

Some of the critical advances in veterinary medicine have been these: vaccination against distemper, rabies, parvovirus, infectious hepatitis, anthrax, tetanus, and feline leukemia; treatment for animal parasites; corrective surgery for hip dysplasia in dogs; orthopedic surgery and rehabilitation for horses; treatment for leukemia and other cancers in pet animals; detection and control of tuberculosis and brucellosis in cattle; control of heartworm infection in dogs;

treatment of arthritis in dogs; protection and preservation of endangered species through vaccinations and improved fertilization. The dean of the Tufts University School of Medicine, Dr. Franklin M. Leow, summarizes the matter forcefully: "Most drugs, diagnostic tests, and surgical techniques used in veterinary medicine today have come either directly from animal research or from human medical or surgical practice that was originally based on animal research." Not for the sake of humans only are animals used in research. If the well-being of animals themselves is to be our concern, research using animals must not be impeded.

Do all these reports of the treating and healing of human beings, and of animals, not give reason enough on any utilitarian calculus to use the mice, or the rabbits, or the chickens such research requires? How many lives must we save, how much agony must we avoid, how much profound human unhappiness must we overcome before all will come to agree that there is little, in science or in any other sphere, that is of more direct and powerful service to humankind, and to animals, than medical research using laboratory animals?

The hopeless effort to ascribe *rights* to animals has been largely abandoned. The claim that mice and chickens have rights as humans do was examined with care in the earlier chapters of this book and shown there to be completely untenable. No satisfactory case can be made for animal rights. Only in a sphere in which moral right and wrong are understood and respected, a human sphere, can agents have rights or do wrongs. "Animal rights" is a popular slogan for the ignorant, but speaking thoughtfully it makes no sense.

Recognizing this, the "animal liberation" movement has shifted emphasis from entitlements to pains, urging that we think not about rights but about *consequences*. Consider the merits and demerits of the alternatives, say they; calculate the balance of goods and evils resulting from animal use; ask whether the gains of research using animals outweigh the losses.

Weighing the Costs and Benefits

Let us do as they ask. Death is inflicted, and some pain, too, on the rats and other animals whose lives are used in medical research. But human death and human pain count at least as much, and probably a good deal more. The misery that humans suffer, and that animals suffer, too, from diseases and disorders now *curable* as the result of laboratory animal research is so great as to be beyond calculation. Add to these what will soon be possible as a result of animal studies now in progress. And put on the scales, in a fair weighing, those medical achievements not yet even well conceived but likely to be realized one day—if research is not crippled by ignorant zealotry. And on the scales put also, with unflinching honesty, all of the horror, and pain, and excruciating misery of human sickness that would certainly have been suffered, and from which we and our children would be suffering now, had animals not been used to bring us to our present circumstances.

Each reader of this book is urged to make this utilitarian calculation. Attend, in fairness, to every bad thing that research with animals entails: its occasional misfires, its risks, the inevitable death of many rodents and rabbits and other animals, and the distress unavoidably caused to some of these creatures. Attend, with equal fairness, to every good thing that research with animals has achieved, is now achieving, and is likely to achieve—every vaccine, every antibiotic, every prosthetic device, every surgical procedure, every successful drug, every advance in medical understanding that has been made possible only by using animals. Consider the saving of lives and the easing of pains that this research has produced. Consider the aims and probable achievements of current research relying on animal use. Consider all the facts, weigh all the arguments carefully, and decide.

Science Helping Animals

DAVID BARBOZA

In the following article, David Barboza of the New York Times *reports on how two traditional enemies of the animal rights movement have started to take animal welfare seriously. According to Barboza, scientists who have long been criticized for experimenting on animals, have begun studying the habits and preferences of domestic animals to determine what makes them happy or content. In turn, Barboza says, such food industry giants as McDonald's, Burger King, KFC, and Wendy's have used the new research to press their suppliers to improve conditions for animals on farms, in transport, and at the slaughterhouse. Barboza notes that even strident animal rights groups, such as People for the Ethical Treatment of Animals, have embraced the changes, although they still urge that more be done.*

The cameras are rolling here at Purdue University's animal research center, tracking a half-dozen pigs, each with an ink streak slathered across its back for identification.

The pigs have a choice to make. They can use their snouts either to let them into a pen where they can socialize with other pigs, or they can stay put with their food.

"We want to get the animal's perspective, to see what they prefer," explains Edmond A. Pajor, assistant professor of animal behavior and welfare at Purdue. "We want to

---

know: How important is social contact and space? What do they like and need?"

A decade ago, big food companies would have dismissed such research as silly, a deviation from the advances in industrial farming that have allowed them to reduce the cost of hamburgers and chicken nuggets. But today, those companies are not just taking the research seriously; they are financing it.

McDonald's, Burger King, KFC and Wendy's have all underwritten research and recently hired what are called animal welfare specialists to help them devise new standards aimed at ensuring more humane treatment of the animals destined for their kitchens. Industry trade groups are promoting the new rules and conducting audits of livestock producers to assure they are being followed, though some groups express concern about higher costs and other complications.

Experts say that the food industry is responding to growing health concerns and criticism of the nation's factory farms, which raise over eight billion animals (mostly chickens) a year in giant production and slaughtering operations. Looming regulations—most immediately in Europe, but also in the United States—are adding to the pressure.

As a result, after decades of crowding more and more animals into smaller and smaller stalls and pens, livestock producers and processors are being asked to create more space for animals, to reduce their reliance on growth-promoting drugs, and to transport and slaughter animals in more humane ways.

Soon, cages might be eliminated from some factory farms, and animals that not long ago were clubbed before being killed—and are now knocked unconscious by electric stun guns—could be first put to sleep gently, with gas.

A New Focus

"The whole drumbeat in the U.S. for the last century has been to reduce the cost of food," said Todd J. Duvick, a food analyst at Banc of America Securities. "Now people are paying attention to things like how food is produced and how animals are treated."

The changes are being applauded even by People for the Ethical Treatment of Animals, or PETA, an organization best known for guerrilla attacks on the fur industry and fast-food outlets, and for publicizing photographs of what they say are cruel acts being performed on animals.

"McDonald's, Burger King and Wendy's have done some pretty good stuff, but they had to be prodded into it," said Dan Shannon, a spokesman for PETA. "These animals are not living in luxury suites being hand-fed grapes, but this is an improvement."

Last week, the McDonald's Corporation said it would begin insisting that its suppliers cut their use of antibiotics in sick animals and eliminate the use of certain growth-promoting antibiotics that are fed to healthy animals, particularly chickens. For several years, health professionals in the United States and Europe have worried that the overuse of antibiotics in farm animals might eventually reduce the medicines' effectiveness in humans.

Health officials applauded McDonald's announcement, but some producers criticized the company for bowing to public pressure and barring the use of some antibiotics that are still deemed safe by regulators.

"The pork industry wants to make sure sound science is driving the industry and not emotion," said Cynthia Cunningham, a spokeswoman for the National Pork Board. "McDonald's is trying to be laudable, but their position was based on marketing."

Whether motivated by marketing concerns or social conscience, McDonald's has stepped to the forefront of the animal welfare movement, at least among corporations.

McDonald's has pressed the egg industry, for instance, to increase by half the amount of space it allocates to egg-laying hens in factory hen houses. The company—which buys two billion eggs a year—has also told its egg suppliers to stop the practice of temporarily withholding food and water to induce hens to lay larger eggs.

Similarly, McDonald's now presses beef suppliers to reduce their use of electrical prods and encourages chicken producers to use automated equipment to gently gather chickens, in place of unskilled laborers who grab birds and stuff them into cages. At slaughterhouses, it insists on boxes that make livestock more comfortable as they are stunned into unconsciousness before being killed.

Setting the Standards

Having established a detailed set of guidelines for the treatment of animals, McDonald's has begun enforcing the standards with random audits of its suppliers. KFC and Burger King are doing the same.

"Essentially, it's the right thing to do," said Chet England, the chief food safety officer at Burger King.

But it is McDonald's, as the world's largest restaurant chain and one of the biggest purchasers of animal products, whose evolving stance is driving change throughout the food industry.

"There will be differences on details, but not on the bigger picture," said Gary Weber, executive director of regulatory affairs at the National Cattlemen's Beef Association. "There might be disagreement on the use of branding, castration or de-horning, and some other matters."

According to McDonald's officials, the turning point in the company's attitudes came in 1997, when executives met for the first time with Temple Grandin, an associate professor at Colorado State University who is an expert in animal behavior and welfare issues.

"We had an interest in this stuff, but couldn't figure it out," said Bob Langert, the senior director of social responsibility at McDonald's. "We went to Colorado State and saw her, and it was magic. She pitched her program, and we thought it was perfect."

Executives found Dr. Grandin's approach "scientific" and

not "emotional," Mr. Langert said. They marveled at her research techniques: how she measured animal behavior and conditions; how she paid attention to animal vocalizations; how she studied their response to electric prods; how she catalogued their adaptations to various conditions.

Indeed, Dr. Grandin often gets down on all fours to walk through a processing plant, as if she were an animal. She has autism, and she says things that bother her because of her condition, like loud noises, can bother animals, as well, McDonald's officials said.

A New Kind of Animal Experimentation

McDonald's has also turned to animal behavior and welfare researchers here at Purdue University, where there are studies looking into such topics as how female pigs socialize and whether cows feel pain when their tails are clipped.

In one research lab, there are jars filled with pig brains and tails lined up on a shelf. Scientists will dissect the specimens to try to determine whether the animals suffered in various experiments run by the lab to simulate factory farm conditions.

Researchers here are also looking at animal handling techniques, barn lighting—almost anything that could cause stress or harm to an animal. They watch hundreds of hours of videotape of animals sleeping, eating, playing and fighting, recording each monotonous detail.

"It's pretty painful to watch those tapes," said Vanessa Kanaan, 22, a first-year Purdue graduate student who is recording piglet behavior on six cameras in a small research cabin. "I look at how they budget their time. Is there cross-suckling? I look at disputes before and after I mix them up. I want to better understand the social effects."

How far animal welfare activists will go in pressing for changes is still unclear. Just yesterday, PETA applauded after David C. Novak, chief executive of Yum Brands—the owner of KFC, Taco Bell, Pizza Hut and other fast-food chains—was doused with a blood-colored substance and stuck with feathers in an animal rights protest in Hanover, Germany.

PETA says that KFC has announced new animal welfare measures but has not gone far enough in carrying them out. Jonathan Blum, a spokesman for Yum, said that KFC recently adopted industry-leading guidelines on animal welfare. He called the attack on the Yum chief an "act of corporate terrorism" that should be prosecuted.

Other big restaurant chains say they are mainly interested in preventing abuse, not creating happier happy meals. "We're not experts on that; we're a restaurant company," said Mr. Langert of McDonald's. "But there are experts in this, and they'll help us draw the line."

Global companies like McDonald's are also being nudged by rulemakers in Europe, where the animal welfare movement has made more headway with government officials.

The European Union has already said by 2012 it will ban the keeping of pregnant pigs in stalls that do not allow room to turn around. In Germany, officials are encouraging pig farmers to give their pigs 20 seconds of human contact each day—and a little tender loving care.

"Pigs should be kept happy with two or three toys to stop them fighting each other, namely toys that have wooden grips or straw dummies," a government official told a newspaper last year. "Every pig must have daylight, and in winter extra lighting should be provided to stop the pigs becoming depressed."

Richard Kirkden, a 34-year-old Purdue postdoctoral student whose expertise is animal motivation, said that his motivation was doing what was right for animals.

"I'm not looking at production, I'm looking at the ethical side," he said. But ethical behavior can have a payoff. "In the U.K., where I come from, people will pay a premium for the better-cared-for animals."

1641

Nathanial Ward of the Massachusetts Bay Colony composes the "Body of Liberties," which forbids "tyranny or cruelty towards any brute creature."

1780

The British philosopher Jeremy Bentham publishes *An Introduction to the Principles of Morals and Legislation*, in which he argues that what matters morally is not whether a being can reason or speak, but whether it can suffer.

1822

The British parliament passes Martin's Act, which makes it illegal to needlessly beat livestock.

1824

The Society for the Prevention of Cruelty to Animals is formed in England. In 1840, Queen Victoria permitted the society to call itself the Royal Society for the Prevention of Cruelty to Animals.

1835

Anticruelty statutes become law in Massachusetts.

1866

Henry Bergh founds the American Society for Prevention of Cruelty to Animals. The society is dedicated to "promoting humane principles, preventing cruelty, and alleviating pain, fear and suffering in all animals."

1877

The American Humane Society is founded.

1882

Caroline Earle White founds the American Anti-Vivisection Society.

1885

The French scientist Louis Pasteur develops a rabies vaccine through his experiments with rabbits and dogs.

1892

The American Humane Association calls for laws banning the repetition of painful experiments for the purpose of teaching well-known or accepted facts.

1907

Every state in the union has an anticruelty statute.

1910

A Massachusetts law to allow the state's Society for the Prevention of Cruelty to Animals to inspect slaughterhouses passes. Vigorous efforts to repeal the law are quashed.

1949

The Metcalf-Hatch Act, which permits researchers to seize unclaimed animals from shelters, is passed in Minnesota, followed by Baltimore and Los Angeles.

1951

Christine Stevens founds the Animal Welfare Institute, which monitors the treatment of research animals.

1958

The Humane Slaughter Act is passed: "No method of slaughter or handling in connection with slaughtering shall be deemed to comply with public policy of the United States unless it is humane."

1959

British researchers William Russell and Rex Burch publish

Principles of Humane Experimental Technique, which leads to the search for alternatives to animal testing.

1963

The Hunt Saboteurs club is founded in Britain. It used direct tactics to interfere with fox hunting. In the United States, the National Institutes of Health develops the first set of guidelines for the care and use of research animals.

1966

The Animal Welfare Act is passed, a U.S. law that authorizes the Secretary of Agriculture to regulate the transport, sale, and handling of dogs, cats, nonhuman primates, guinea pigs, hamsters, and rabbits intended for research.

1970

The Animal Welfare Act is extended to cover most warm-blooded animals.

1971

The United States Department of Agriculture excludes mice, rats, and birds from coverage under the Animal Welfare Act.

1972

The Animal Liberation Front, a radical animal rights group, is founded in Britain. In the thirty years since its founding, the loosely knit organization has been responsible for thousands of "direct action" campaigns, which range from vandalism promoting an animal rights message to break-ins at major research labs, where lab animals are removed and scientific equipment destroyed.

1975

The Austrailian philosopher Peter Singer publishes *Animal Liberation*, which argues that the interests of animals deserve equal consideration with humans. Henry Spira, a prominent animal rights activist, leads a protest against the

Museum of Natural History in New York and succeeds in stopping research involving cats.

1979

Spira leads a successful lobbying effort to repeal the Metcalf-Hatch Act.

1980

Revlon, responding to pressure from Spira, stops using the Draize test, which involves putting inflammatory substances into the eyes of albino rabbits.

1981

Police raid the Institute for Behavioral Research in Silver Spring, Maryland, and press seventeen charges against Edward Taub for cruelty to animals. Alex Pacheco, one of the founders of People for the Ethical Treatment of Animals, had been working undercover in the lab and tipped off police.

1983

The British philosopher Mary Midgeley publishes *Animals and Why They Matter.*

1984

People for the Ethical Treatment of Animals raids Thomas Gennarelli's lab at the University of Pennsylvania and releases video footage to the public showing cruel experiments on baboons. The philosopher Tom Regan publishes *In Defense of Animals*, a book many consider to be the leading account of the philosophical basis of animal rights. DNA research shows humans and chimpanzees are more closely related to each other than either of them are to any of the other great apes.

1985

Congress amends the Animal Welfare Act, mandating that

experimental procedures minimize animal suffering with appropriate anesthesia, analgesics, and euthanasia.

1986

The philosopher Michael Allen Fox publishes *The Case for Animal Experimentation*, a seminal book defending research on animals.

1987

Revlon agrees to stop all animal testing and to contribute millions of dollars to animal research.

1991

The first transgenic sheep, named Tracey, is born. She has human genes that let her produce human protein in her milk.

1995

The first baboon-to-human bone marrow transplant is performed on an AIDS patient.

1996

The first world congress on alternatives to animal experimentation is held in the Netherlands.

1997

British scientists successfully clone a sheep, which they name Dolly.

Organizations to Contact

The editors have compiled the following list of organizations concerned with the topics contained in this book. The descriptions are derived from materials provided by the organizations. All have publications or information available for interested readers. The list was compiled on the date of publication of the present volume; the information provided here may change. Be aware that many organizations take several weeks or longer to respond to inquiries, so allow as much time as possible.

American Anti-Vivisection Society (AAVS)
801 Old York Rd. #204, Jenkintown, PA 19046-1685
(215) 887-0816 • (800) SAY-AAVS • fax: (215) 887-2088
Web site: www.aavs.org • e-mail: aavs@aavs.org

The AAVS is an international organization that works to end vivisection (the use of animals in research, dissection, testing, and education). The group contends that vivisection actually harms people as well as animals by wasting time, effort, and money on research of little or no benefit, while nonanimal, scientific research holds great promise for both human and animal ailments. *The Cruel Deception* is one of many books published by AAVS. They also make available numerous reports, brochures, and videos.

Americans for Medical Progress (AMP)
908 King St., Suite 301, Alexandria, VA 22314
(703) 836-9595 • fax: (703) 836-9594
Web site: www.ampef.org/ • e-mail: info@amprogress.org

AMP is a nonprofit organization that works to raise public awareness and education regarding medical research with animals and its importance to curing today's most devastating diseases. Its Web site has current listings of articles in the media regarding the use of animals in research, as well as fact sheets and handouts.

Animal Alliance of Canada
221 Broadview Ave., Suite 101, Toronto, ON M4M 2G3 Canada
(416) 462-9541 • fax: (416) 462-9647
Web site: www.animalalliance.ca
e-mail: info@animalalliance.ca

The Animal Alliance of Canada is an animal rights advocacy and education group which focuses on local, regional, national, and international issues concerning the goodwill and respectful treatment of animals by humans. Animal Alliance investigates the conditions under which millions of animals suffer each day using industry contracts, unannounced visits, literature surveys, and freedom of information legislation. Its findings are published in fact sheets and in its *Take Action* newsletter.

Animal League Defense Fund (ALDF)
127 Fourth St., Petaluma, CA 94952-3005
(707) 769-7771 • fax: (707) 769-0785
Web site: www.aldf.org • e-mail: info@aldf.org

ALDF is an organization of attorneys and law students who promote animal rights and protect the lives and interests of animals through the use of their legal skills. It publishes the Animals' Advocate quarterly.

Animal Rights Law Center, Rutgers University
Rutgers Law School
123 Washington St., Newark, New Jersey 07102
fax: (973) 353-1445 • Web site: www.animal-law.org

The center is run by Gary Francione, an active figure in the animal rights movement. The center maintains records of legal decisions concerning animal rights and offers support to students who refuse to experiment on animals in school.

Animal Welfare Institute (AWI)
PO Box 3650, Washington, DC 20027
(703) 836-4300 • fax: (703) 836-0400
Web site: www.awionline.org

The AWI is a nonprofit charitable organization founded in 1951 to reduce the sum total of pain and fear inflicted on animals by humans. It advocates the humane treatment of laboratory animals and the development and use of non-animal testing methods as well as encourages humane science teaching and prevention of painful experiments on animals by high school students. The AWI publications include the books *Beyond the Laboratory Door* and *The Principles of Humane Experimental Technique*, and the newsletter *AWI Quarterly*.

Farm Animal Reform Movement (FARM)
PO Box 30654, Bethesda, MD 20824
(800) ask-farm
Web site: www.farmusa.org

FARM seeks to moderate and eliminate animal suffering and other adverse impacts of commercial animal production. It promotes the annual observance of March 20th as "The Great American Meatout," a day of meatless meals, and provides a variety of brochures and fact sheets for consumers and activists.

Food Animal Concerns Trust (FACT)
PO Box 14599, Chicago, IL 60614
(312) 525-4952 • fax: (312) 525-5226
Web site: www.fact.cc • e-mail: info@fact.cc

FACT promotes better care of farm animals and improved farming methods to produce safer foods, and focuses on the food safety problems that arise from intensive animal production. Believing that factory-farming methods should be abolished, FACT helps farmers fund operations that raise animals humanely. Its trademarks are Nest Eggs and Rambling Rose Brand free-range veal. It publishes a quarterly newsletter, FACT Acts, as well as fact sheets and numerous brochures and pamphlets.

Foundation for Biomedical Research
818 Connecticut Ave. NW, Suite 303, Washington, DC 20006
(202) 457-0654
Web site: www.fbresearch.org • e-mail: info@fbresearch.org

This organization runs public education programs on the importance of animal research for the treatment of human disease. It has a speaker's bureau and public relations programs, and bills itself as "a formal opposition to animal rights activists."

Incurably Ill for Animal Research
PO Box 27454, Lansing, MI 48909
(517) 887-1550
Web site: www.iifar.org • e-mail: info@iifar.org

This organization consists of people who have incurable diseases and are concerned that the use of animals in medical research will be stopped or severely limited by animal rights activists, thus delaying or preventing the development of new cures. It publishes the monthly *Bulletin* and a quarterly newsletter.

Institute for In Vitro Sciences (IIVS)
21 Firstfield Rd., Suite 220, Gaithersburg, MD 20878
(301) 947-6523 • fax: (301) 947-6538
Web site: www.iivs.org

IIVS is a nonprofit, technology-driven, foundation for the advancement of alternative methods to animal testing. In order to facilitate the reduction of animal use in testing, the Institute promotes the optimization, use, and acceptance of *in vitro* methodologies worldwide. IIVS makes its published articles available on its Web site.

Johns Hopkins Center for Alternatives to Animal Testing (CAAT)
111 Market Pl., Suite 840, Baltimore, MD 21202-6709
(410) 223-1693 • fax: (410) 223-1603
Web site: http://caat.jhsph.edu/ • e-mail: caat@jhsph.edu

CAAT fosters the development of scientifically acceptable alternatives to animal testing for use in the development and safety evaluation of commercial and therapeutic products. The center conducts symposia for researchers and corporations. Its publications include Alternative Methods in Toxicology, Animals and Alternatives in Testing, and a periodic newsletter.

National Anti-Vivisection Society
53 West Jackson Blvd., Suite 1552, Chicago, IL 60604-3795
(312) 427-6065 • (800) 888-6287 • (800) 922-FROG
Web site: www.navs.org • e-mail: feedback@navs.org

This group, founded in 1929, campaigns against animal experimentation. Its dissection hotline offers information on alternatives to dissection and it loans teachers and students hand-painted, anatomically correct three-dimensional models of frogs and fetal pigs.

People for the Ethical Treatment of Animals (PETA)

501 Front St., Norfolk, VA 23510
(757) 622-PETA (7382) • fax: (757) 622-0457
Web site: www.peta.org • e-mail: info@peta.org

An international animal rights organization, PETA is dedicated to establishing and protecting the rights of animals. If focuses on four areas: factory farms, research laboratories, the fur trade, and the entertainment industry. PETA promotes public education, cruelty investigations, animal rescue, celebrity involvement, and legislative and direct action. It produces numerous videos and publishes *Animal Times*, various fact sheets, brochures, and flyers.

Tufts Center for Animals and Public Policy

Tufts University School of Veterinary Medicine
200 Westboro Rd. North, Grafton, MA 01536
(508) 839-7991
Web site: www.tufts.edu/vet/cfa/

The center supports conferences exploring animals and public policy and publishes two newsletters, *Animals and Public Policy* and the *Alternatives Report.*

For Further Research

Books

Deborah Blum, *The Monkey Wars*. New York: Oxford University Press, 1994. The author won a Pulitzer Prize for the *Sacramento Bee* newspaper articles that she later developed into this book exploring the controversy over experiments on primates.

David C. Coats and Michael W. Fox, *Old MacDonald's Factory Farm: The Myth of the Traditional Farm and the Shocking Truth About Animal Suffering in Today's Agribusiness*. New York: Continuum, 1986. This book explores the rise of large scale farming operations and their impact on animal welfare.

Michael Allen Fox, *The Case for Animal Experimentation: An Evolutionary and Ethical Perspective*. Berkeley: University of California, 1986. Although the author later retracted his views and is currently an advocate of animal rights, this book is one of the central texts defending animal experimentation.

Michael W. Fox, *Superpigs and Wondercorn: The Brave New World of Biotechnology and Where It All May Lead*. New York: Lyons and Burford, 1992. This book strongly criticizes emerging biotechnologies such as genetic engineering.

Gary Francione, *Animals, Property, and the Law*. Philadelphia: Temple University Press, 1995. Francione (a law professor at Rutgers) offers a historical analysis of the status of animals as legal property and an illuminating discussion of the importance of the distinction between animal welfare and animal rights.

Raymond Frey, *Interests and Rights: The Case Against Animals*. New York: Oxford University, 1980. The author argues that animals do not have beliefs and desires because they do not have language, and that this means they have no rights.

Silvio Garattini and D.W. Bekkum, eds., *The Importance of Animal Experimentation for Safety and Biomedical Research*. Boston: Kluwer Academic, 1990. This anthology defends the importance of animals to scientific research.

Robert Garner, ed., *Animal Rights: The Changing Debate*. New York: New York University, 1997. This anthology of recent essays addresses the increased radicalism within the animal rights movements.

Stanley Godlovitch, Rosalind Godlovitch, and John Harris, eds., *Animals, Men, and Morals: An Inquiry into the Maltreatment of Non-Humans*. New York: Traplinger, 1971. The philosopher Peter Singer describes this collection of thirteen essays as the manifesto for animal liberation.

Michael Leahy, *Against Liberation: Putting Animals in Perspective*. New York: Routlege, 1994. The author is against animal rights, saying that animals in captivity typically have better lives than animals in the wild.

Finn Lynge, *Arctic Wars, Animal Rights, Endangered People*. Hanover, NH: University Press of New England, 1992. The author addresses the conflict between the rights of animals and the rights of indigenous people to hunt and fish.

Tom Regan, *The Case for Animal Rights*. Berkeley: University of California, 1985. In a book many consider the most sophisticated defense of animal rights, the author argues animals have moral rights because they have "inherent value."

Bernard Rollin, *Animal Rights and Human Morality*. Buffalo, NY: Prometheus Books, 1992. In the first chapter, the author, who is both a scientist and a philosopher, presents an excellent summary of various philosophical positions in regard to animal rights.

Roger Scruton, *Animal Rights and Wrongs*. London: Demos, 1996. The author, a British philosopher, argues animals do not have rights.

Peter Singer, *Animal Liberation: A New Ethic for Our Treatment of Animals*. New York: New York Review of Books, 1990. The original edition of this book, published in 1975, is often credited as having started the modern animal rights movement.

Rod Strand and Patti Strand, *The Hijacking of the Humane Movement: Animal Extremism*. Wilsonville, OR: Doral, 1983. The authors, who are dog breeders, harshly criticize animal rights supporters.

Periodicals

Sharon Begley and Mary Hager, "Liberation in the Labs," *Newsweek*, August 27, 1984. This article reports that, as of 1984, animal rights groups in the United States were gaining respect and support.

Betsy Carpenter, "Upsetting the Ark," *U.S. News & World Report*, August 24, 1992. Carpenter reports on how by the early 1990s zoos were under increasing public pressure to justify their keeping animals captive.

Peter Gwynne, with Sharon Begley, "Animals in the Lab," *Newsweek*, March 27, 1978. This article reports on the rising concern with animal experimentation.

Terence Monmany and Mary Hager, "Should Man Make Beast?" *Newsweek*, May 4, 1987. This article reports on public concerns over the genetic engineering of animals.

Michael Satschell, "The American Hunter Under Fire," *U.S. News & World Report*, February 5, 1990. This article is about the controversy surrounding hunting in the United States.

————, "Terrorize People, Save Animals," *U.S. News & World Report*, April 8, 2002. Satschell reports on an extended, intense effort by animal rights activists to shut down Huntingdon Life Sciences, a biomedical testing laboratory, by force and intimidation.

Dave Shiflett, "Take a Fish to Lunch: But You Better Not Eat It, Says PETA," *American Spectator*, December 1997. Shiflett reports how, by 1997, animal rights activists were targeting both anglers and the commercial fish industry.

Michael Specter, "The Extremist: The Woman Behind the Most Successful Radical Group in America," *New Yorker*, April 14, 2003. This lengthy articles profiles Ingrid Newkirk, one of the founders of People for the Ethical Treatment of Animals.

Cass A. Sunstein, "Slaughterhouse Jive," *New Republic*, January 29, 2001. This article is a lengthy review of Gary Francione's *Introduction to Animal Rights: Your Child or Your Dog?*

Steven Zak, "Ethics and Animals," *Atlantic Monthly*, March 1989. This lengthy article offers an overview of the various philosophical positions for and against animal rights.

agriculture, 16
American Humane Society, 18
American National Cancer
   Institute, 183–84
Ames test, 182
anesthesia, 38, 39, 52, 57
Animal Diagnostic Lab, UC
   Davis, 157
animal experimentation
   accomplishments from,
      134–35
   animal feelings and, 37–39
   case scenario for
      justification of, 128–29
   cosmetics testing and,
      185–86
   disturbing images in
      videotapes of, 128
   exaggeration of pain and
      torture with, 52–53
   examples of, 138–40
   finding a moral justification
      for, 144–45
   getting rid of, 143–44
   goals of activists on, 146
   historical impact of, 189–91
   history of debate on, 179–80
   humane societies visiting
      laboratories of, 57–58
   human superiority and,
      39–41
   improving welfare of factory
      farm animals with, 195–200
   laws restricting, 44, 46–47,
      59
   medical progress from,
      55–56, 137–38, 191–92
   1975 investigation into, 23
   opposition to, 18, 51–52
      costs associated with
         action of, 159
      interferes with science,
         54–55
      lab raids
         during 1980s, 150–57
         during 1999, 159–60
      misleading claims by, 53–54
      success of, 135, 140–41
   reform in, 141–43, 180–82
   rules and regulations used
      for, 56–57
   selfishness of, 39
   torture of animals and,
      36–37
   using illegal means to stop,
      justification for, 163–67
   using lawful means to stop,
      165–66
   value and significance of, 58
   veterinary medicine benefits
      from, 192–93
   weighing costs and benefits
      of, 194
animal fighting, 43, 46
Animal Liberation (Singer),
   19–20, 25
   as a bible for the animal
      rights movement, 62–63
   contents of, 64–65
   impact of, 65, 122

Animal Liberation Front
(ALF), 22, 136
lab raids by, 150–60
violent tactics by, 23–24, 169,
175–77
animal products, 64
animal rights
animal welfare is a slippery
slope to, 121
do not make sense, 193
historical development of,
28–30
human rights and, 34,
130–31
need for comprehensive
principle on, 30–31
rise of, to prominence, 15
animal rights activism/
activists
on animal experimentation
reform, 143
disturbing images in
videotapes of, 126–27, 128
issues of, 136–37
lack of extremism in, 119–21
must adhere to nonviolence,
168–70
reasons for activism by, 122
should not destroy property,
170–71
stereotypes about, 121–22
tactics of, 136
terrorist links to, 173–75
mainstream support for,
175–77
unlawful means used by,
165–66
justification for, 166–67
see also animal
experimentation,
opposition to; animal
rights movement

Animal Rights Militia, 157
animal rights movement
animal welfare movement
vs., 121
goals of, 88, 146–49
growing number of groups
in, 135
historical development of,
17, 18–19, 22–26, 72–74
impact of philosophers on,
70–71
progress in, 131–32
role of philosophers in,
61–62
Animal Rights Network, 146
animals
are not our resources, 88–89
awareness in, 110–11
compared with humans,
78–80
contractarian view of, 91–92
cruelty-kindness view of,
92–93
denial of feelings in, 32–33
equality of, with humans,
63–64, 74–78
rationality and, 106–108
evidence for pain and
sensations in, 111–13
evolutionary argument for
pain in, 113–14
fear in, 117–18
historical perception of,
15–16
humans vs., 144–45
improving conditions for
factory farm, 195–200
indirect duties view of,
89–90
inherent worth of, 67–68,
98–99
drawing lines between

types of animals for,
103–105
obscurity of, 101–103
insensitive treatment of
lack of justification for,
33–34
religious reasons for, 31–32
interpreting mental lives of,
109–10
killing vs. harming, 80–81
moral inequality of, with
humans, 84, 85–86
moral value of, 103–104
used in entertaining, 43, 46,
148–49
Animals Film, The (PETA
video), 126–27
Animals, Men, and Morals
(Godlovitch), 19
Animal Welfare Act, 1985
amendments to, 141, 142–43
antibiotics, 197
anticruelty laws. *See*
legislation
anxiety, 115–17
Aquinas, Thomas, 73
Aristotle, 16–17, 107
arson, 157–58, 162, 176

baboons, 128
Barboza, David, 195
Baylor College of Medicine,
137
Bentham, Jeremy, 21, 30, 63,
75–77
Bergh, Henry, 18
Between the Species (journal),
69
Bick, Katherine, 143
biotechnology, 24–25, 149
Blaauboer, Bas, 187
Boothe, Ronald, 138

Brophy, Brigid, 19
Buddhist thought, 73
Burger King, 196, 198

California law, 49
Californians for Responsible
Research, 70
Cal State Sacramento, 152
Cannon, Walter Bradford, 51
Case for Animal Rights, The
(Regan), 22, 67, 68–69
cats, used in research
investigation into, 23
lab raids and, 155
misleading claims on, 53–54
opposition to, 134–35
cell-culture methods, 183–84
Chimpanzee Politics (de
Waal), 127
chimpanzees, 127–28, 129,
141–42, 143
Christian views, on animals,
16, 31–32, 73, 83
City of Hope cancer research
labs, 152–53
classical rights theory, 22
Cohen, Carl, 189
Colorado law, 49
Combes, Robert, 187
Committee for the Protection
of Medical Research, 59
Cornell University, 134–35
cosmetics testing, 181
cruelty, 93
Culture and Animals
Foundation, 67

Darwin, Charles, 33
DeGrazia, David, 109
DEREK (software), 186
Descartes, René, 32–33
de Waal, Frans, 127

DNA, 85
dogs, 46
Draize test, 23, 142, 185

Economist (magazine), 179
economy, 25–26
education, animal welfare, 48–50
egalitarianism, 94
Emory University, 136, 138
England. *See* Great Britain
Enlightenment, 17, 29
Environmental Liberation Front (ELF), 174, 175–76
Ethics (journal), 69
Ethics and Animals (journal), 69
Etyka (journal), 69
Europe, 181, 200
Expanding Circle, The (Singer), 129–30

farming, factory, 147
improving animal conditions for, 195–200
fast-food chains, 196–200
Ferrara Meat Company, 157
firebombings, 157–58
fish, 104
food industry, 196–200
Francione, Gary, 25–26
fur coats, 131, 148

game species management, 148
Gandhi, Mohandas, 66, 169, 172
Gennarelli, Thomas, 150–51
genetic engineering, 24–25
God, granting humans dominion over animals, 18–19

Godlovitch, Roslind, 19
Godlovitch, Stanley, 19
Goodall, Jane, 143
Gordon-Lickey, Barbara, 155
gorillas, 127
Grandin, Temple, 198–99
Great Britain
animal experimentation reform in, 180
animal rights essays in, 29–30
anticruelty laws in, 17–18, 42–44
initial reaction to animal rights movement in, 73–74
organizations in, 23
protests on animal experimentation in, 179–80
second phase of animal rights movement in, 19–20
Greenpeace, 23

Harris, John, 19
Harvard Medical School, 136
Hayward Friends of Animals, 70
Hindu thought, 73
Howard University, 152
Humane Farming Association, 70
Humane Society of the United States, 176
human rights, 129–31, 132
humans
equality among, 75
as masters over animals, 16–17
moral inequality and, 84–86
Huntingdon Life Sciences, 174–75
Hunt Sabateurs Association, 23

Illinois, 47, 49
immortality
    human vs. animal, 31–32
    inherent value and, 98
In Defense of Animals, 70
Inquiry (journal), 69
insects, 104, 114
Institute for Behavior
    Research, 140
Intelligence Report (Southern
    Poverty Law Center), 174,
    175–76
invertebrate animals, 104, 114

Jameson, Ann, 31
Jasper, James M., 61
Johns Hopkins University, 152

Katz, Elliot, 70
Kentucky Fried Chicken
    (KFC), 196, 198
kindness, 92–93
King, Martin Luther, Jr., 169,
    172

LD-50 test, 142
legislation
    on animal experimentation,
        46–47
    on animal welfare education,
        48–50
    in European countries, 44
    in Great Britain, 17–18,
        42–44, 59, 73–74
    interferes with science, 54
    on neglect, 47
    on transportation and
        disposal of animals, 48
    in United States, 44–47

Mahoney, James, 141–42
Maine, 49

Martin's Act (1822), 17–18, 43
Massachusetts, 47
McCrea, Roswell, 42
McDonald's, 196, 197–98
mental capacities, 164–65
mentally retarded persons,
    161–62, 164–65
Michigan, 47
microbes, 182–83
microfauna, 104
Middle Ages, 29
Midgley, Mary, 69
Miller, Brad, 70
Monist, The (journal), 69
monkeys, experiments
    involving, 137, 139, 140,
    163–64
monoclonal antibodies, 183
Montana, 49
"Moral Basis of
    Vegetarianism, The"
    (Regan), 66
morality
    contractarian view of, 90–92
    indirect duties view of,
        89–90
    kindness-cruelty view of,
        92–93
    rights view of, 96–97
moral rights/status
    animal vs. human
        inequality in, 84, 85–86
        problems with equality of,
            100–101
        Singer on, 21–22, 62–63
    drawing distinction between
        types of animals for,
        103–105
    growing preoccupation with,
        135
    idea of, development of,
        129–30

lack of connection between inherent value and, 102
rationality and, 20, 105–108
sentience matters to, 123–24
uniquely human attributes and, 124–25

National Institutes of Health, 23
National Research Council, 144
Nelkin, Dorothy, 61
New Hampshire, 49–50
Newkirk, Ingrid, 119–20, 122, 140–41, 143
Newsweek (magazine), 134
New York, 45–46, 49
New York University Medical Center, 152
Nobel Prize, 190–91
No Compromise (magazine), 150
North Dakota, 49

Okamoto, Michiko, 134–35
Oklahoma, 47
Orem, John, 159

Pacheco, Alex, 120, 122, 140
pain
  behavioral evidence of, in animals, 111–12
  denying ability for animals to feel, 37–39
  evolutionary argument for evidence of, in animals, 113–14
  in invertebrates, 114
  physiological evidence of, in animals, 112–13
  suffering vs., 115
  see also sentience; suffering

Paine, Thomas, 29–30
paleolithic cave paintings, 15
Palo Alto Humane Society, 136
Peace-making Among Primates (de Waal), 127
Pennsylvania, 44–45, 47, 49
People for the Ethical Treatment of Animals (PETA), 151
  affiliation of, with terrorist activities, 175–76
  on factory farm improvements, 197, 199–200
  formation of, 23
Philosophy (journal), 69
physiologically based biokinetic model (PBBK), 187
pigs, 195–96
politics, 130
Porphyry, 28–29
Primate Research Center, Madison, Wisconsin, 139
primates, 127–28, 129
  see also chimpanzees; monkeys
primitive cultures, 15–16
Purdue University, 195–96

quantitative structure activity relationships (QSARs), 186

rabbits, 137–38, 142, 185
rationality, 20, 105–108, 145
Regan, Tom, 22, 87
  on the inherent worth of animals, 67–68
  political/philosophical influences on, 66–67
  response to book by, 68
  Singer and, 69

strong animal rights
  argument made by, 100–101
religion, 31–32
reptiles, 104
research
  alternatives to using animals
    for, 182–85
  decreasing need for animals
    in, 180, 181
  using computer models for,
    186–88
  using illegal methods to
    stop, 161–63
  see also animal
  experimentation
rhesus monkeys, 137
"Rights of Man" (Paine), 29
rights view, 96–97
Romanes, George, 32–33
Ryder, Richard, 19

Salt, Henry, 28
Sanderson, Derek, 186
San Jose Meat Company, 157
San Jose Veal Company
  warehouse, 157
Sapontzis, Steve, 69–70
Schering Agrochemicals, 186
Sema, Inc., 143
sentience, 110
  in invertebrates, 114
  motivates animal rights
    activism, 122–24
  see also pain; suffering
Serpell, James, 15–16
Shaftesbury, Lord, 19
Siegel, Steve, 135
Simonelli, Jerry, 168
Simonsen Labs, 159
Singer, Peter, 72, 161
  on animal experimentation,
    138–40

argument made by, 20–22,
  25, 62–63
book on animal rights by,
  19–20
impact of, 62–63
on equality of animals and
  humans, 63–64
on illegal tactics, 161–67
impact of, on animal rights
  movement, 65
on Judeo-Christian ethic, 83
utilitarian perspective of, 63
rejection of, 65–66
Sivak, Jacob, 185
Skin 2, 184–85
Smith, Wesley J., 173
Society for the Prevention of
  Cruelty to Animals, 18
Society for the Study of Ethics
  and Animals, 69
South Africa, 130–31
South Dakota, 49
Southern Poverty Law Center
  (SPLC), 174, 175–76
speciesism, 20, 63, 64, 76, 164
Spira, Henry, 23
Stanford University, 136
Sterling, Charles, 128
Stop Huntingdon Animal
  Cruelty (SHAC), 169, 174
suffering
  capacity for, animal equality
    and, 77
  evidence for, in animals, 118
  by humans vs. animals,
    125–26
  as issue for animal products
    and experimentation, 64
  treating animal suffering as
    our own, 82–83

Texas, 49

Timberlake, William, 82
Trans-Species Unlimited, 135
Trull, Frankie, 137

UCLA Harbor Medical Center, 152
United States
  animal experimentation reform in, 181
  anticruelty laws in, 44–47
University of Arizona, Tucson, 157–59
University of California, Berkeley, 152
University of California, Davis, 157
University of California, Riverside, 154
University of California School of Medicine, Davis, 137
University of Florida, 152
University of Maryland, 152
University of Massachusetts, 152
University of Minnesota, 159
University of Oregon, Eugene, 155
University of Pennsylvania, 150–51, 152
University of Pennsylvania Vet School, 151
University of Southern

Florida, 152
U.S. Naval Medical Research Institute, 152
utilitarianism, 63
  alternative theory to, 96–97
  on equality, 75–76
  moral principles of, 93–94
  problems with, 94–96
  rejection of, 65–66, 67–68

vegetarianism, 24, 147
veterinary medicine, 192–93
"Vindication of the Rights of Women" (Wollstonecraft), 29–30
vivisection. *See* animal experimentation

Warren, Mary Anne, 100
Washington, 47, 49
Wendy's, 196
Widdrington, Enid, 35
Wollstonecraft, Mary, 29–30
Wood, J.G., 33
Wright, Robert, 119
Wyoming, 49

Xenometrix, 184

Yerkes Regional Primate Research Center, 136, 138